The Cubist Theatre

Studies in the Fine Arts
The Avant-Garde, No. 38

Stephen C. Foster, Series Editor

Associate Professor of Art History
University of Iowa

Other Titles in This Series

The Cubist Theatre

by
J. Garrett Glover

UMI RESEARCH PRESS
Ann Arbor, Michigan

Produced and distributed by
UMI Research Press
an imprint of
University Microfilms International
Ann Arbor, Michigan 48106

Library of Congress Cataloging in Publication Data

Glover, J. Garrett (Joseph Garrett)
    The cubist theatre.

        (Studies in fine arts. The avant-garde ; no. 38)
        Revision of thesis (Ph.D.)—New York University, 1980.
        Bibliography: p.
        Includes index.
        1. Theater—Production and direction. 2. Cubism—
    Influence. 3. Theater—History—20th century. 4. Theaters
    —Stage-setting and scenery.   I. Title. II. Series: Studies in
    the fine arts. Avant-garde ; no. 38.
    PN2039.G54 1983   792'.023   83-3631
    ISBN 0-8357-1439-X

To my mother and father and the memory of M

Contents

List of Plates

Acknowledgments

I am grateful to all of those people who have contributed in large and small part to the completion of this book. Single thanks belong to Michael Kirby, distinguished scholar and artist, for his encouragement and guidance throughout the development of this study. In addition, I thank the editors, clerks, friends, relatives, teachers and collectors, especially Mr. and Mrs. N. Lobanov-Rostovsky in this last category, for their enthusiastic support of the project.

Introduction

The importance of Cubism to the art and values of the twentieth century has been a popular thesis over the past fifty or sixty years. Cubism has been variously referred to as "the classicism of modern art,"[1] a response to the "critical artistic problems of the twentieth century,"[2] the origin of all modern abstract art, "an oblique guide to the values that preceded as well as survived the movement,"[3] a convention "underlying all realms of contemporary thinking,"[4] and a reflection of "the leading insight of the 20th Century...."[5]

Cubism has been given importance because it has been considered the pictorial expression of the most influential philosophy of this century: the theory of relativity. The philosophy of relativity maintained that man did not objectively perceive the world but invented reality while he perceived it. The Cubist painters translated mental impressions of the world into images that bore only a slight resemblance to visual reality. Picasso spoke for his colleagues when he said, "I paint objects as I think them, not as I see them."[6]

Cubism was an expression of subjective perception, of a conceived reality, and did not advance an ideology, a social cause, or any other intellectual or political concern. Cubism was simply an aesthetic dissection of nature and the visual image; according to Georges Braque, the Cubist painters were not concerned with the "reconstitution" of an anecdotal fact but with the "constitution" of a pictorial fact.[7] Cubism was, to Juan Gris, a "pictorial technique"[8] in which pictorial forms expressed an interior understanding of reality derived from the artist's interaction with the objects of his environment. This interaction was expressed in the formalistic fusion of space and form, in a flattened, two-dimensional pictorial treatment of the world.

Cubism was an aesthetic pursuit, its stylistic innovations quickly adopted by the other arts, particularly architecture, industrial art, music, poetry, and literature. Cubism also had an impact on the theatre, although little has been written about Cubist aesthetics and theatrical production.

Most studies have been limited to an analysis of the Cubist costume design and stage decor, and have overlooked the use of Cubist devices in choreography, blocking, movement, and other aspects of production.[9]

If Cubism has had as great an effect on the arts and values of this century as some historians claim, then it seems reasonable to assume that Cubism has had a greater effect on twentieth-century theatre than the few limited reports suggest; the impact of Cubism has affected not only costume and scene design but approaches and methods by which directors organized all scenic elements, including lighting, choreography and movement, actor groupings, etc.; it seems feasible to refer to a *Cubistic mise-en-scène.*

After 1913, when Cubist pictorial devices first appeared on stage, several theatricians, most of them working in the Russian theatre, created a style of staging that resembled Cubist painting. It is these productions that constitute the *Cubist Theatre.*

The point of this study is not to suggest that the Cubist Theatre was practiced by a specific group of individuals who pooled their talents and ideas to form a school or movement; the point is first to acknowledge the vast influence of Cubism on twentieth-century arts and culture, then to discuss the various ways this influence was manifested in theatrical productions. For this study it is necessary to precisely define and explain a Cubist aesthetics, to extract from theoretical and critical essays the practical techniques and style that eventually defined Cubism, to analyze photographic and written documents of productions that appear Cubistic, then, finally, to explain the extent to which these productions were Cubistic.

The study is not an attempt to analyze every production which displayed Cubistic features. It focuses only on selected early Cubist productions because the intent is to reveal the different ways Cubist devices were employed in the theatre, not to present a chronology or history of Cubist staging; only the early productions are significant because they act as precedents for subsequent Cubist productions.

To provide an historical framework for the discussion, the study begins with Kasimir Malevich's creations for *Victory Over the Sun* — here referred to as the first instance of Cubism on stage — and Pablo Picasso's designs for *Parade* — which has traditionally been recognized as the theatrical debut of Cubism. In the interval between these two productions, Natalia Goncharova and Mikhail Larionov designed Cubistic set pieces and costumes for *Le Coq d'Or* and *Le Chout,* respectively. These productions exhibit the most rudimentary way in which a Cubist aesthetics was applied to theatrical production: primarily in the scenography and costume design, and secondarily in special effects. In this way, these chapters provide a formalistic, as well as an historical, basis for the discussion of subsequent productions.

Several productions by Vsevolod Meyerhold and Alexander Tairov are included because their work reveals the manifold theatrical practicability of Cubist pictorial devices. The study contains an analysis of the following Meyerhold productions: *Mystery Bouffe, The Dawns, The Magnificent Cuckold, The Death of Tarelkin, The Forest,* and *Give Us Europe.* The following Tairov productions are discussed: *Famira Kifared, L'Annonce Faite à Marie,* and *Phaedre.*

Cubist artist Fernand Léger is included because he created Cubist designs for the Swedish Ballet, and, through published and unpublished essays, developed a plan or theory for a *theatre of spectacle.*

1

A Definition of Cubism

Cubism: The Evolution of a Conceived Reality

Cubism evolved out of Post-Impressionism. It was primarily Paul Cézanne who furnished the Cubist painters with a model for perceiving the world and portraying the interaction among objects in space. Cézanne exaggerated form and structure in an effort to reveal the underlying and elemental construction of perceived objects. He modestly enhanced volumes, planes, and geometric qualities of objects and lifted them out of a conventional perspective into a context of pure form. The division between form and space was diminished slightly in his paintings because the forms of objects were often formally integrated with the space around them. Diminishing the division between object and environs, Cézanne anticipated the more radical treatment the Cubists were to give to object/field, foreground/background interrelationships.

Accentuating the architectonic features of objects, Cézanne was the first painter to consider form independent of the subject, an innovation Picasso experimented with in his pre-Cubist works, then went on to develop in his Cubist renderings. Comparing Cézanne's *Boy in the Red Vest* (1895) and Picasso's *Nude Girl with Long Hair* (1906), Paul Schwartz notices that both painters distorted the subject to describe its formal presence.[1] Although Picasso's painting contained a more radical distortion than Cézanne's, both artists altered the anatomical features and proportions of the subjects in order to accentuate their architectonic construction.

It was principally Picasso and Braque who developed Cézanne's experiments with form and space, and it has been generally thought that the early history of Cubism was the history of the friendship between the painters. Picasso and Braque continued Cézanne's modification of the perceptual logic in Renaissance paintings and favored Cézanne's conceptual, formalistic treatment of perspective and space. They were the originators of the stylistic idiosyncracies of Cubism, including collage, typographical inclusions on the picture surface, and the use of found objects.

When Picasso combined simultaneity with the planar formalism of African art in *Les Demoiselles d'Avignon* (1907), he abandoned Renaissance norms involving figure style and one-point perspective and presented the first glimpse of the excessive geometricization that both he and Braque later developed in their paintings of 1908. Braque painted an assemblage of buildings in *Houses at L'Estaque* (1908) and ignored the perceptual logic of the house-in-space. He fabricated a perspective, a conceived perspective, in the stacked geometric cubes and volumes that described the buildings. Picasso painted a similar picture at Horta de San Juan at about the same time. Braque's *Houses at L'Estaque* and Picasso's rendering of houses at Horta de San Juan were considered retrospectively "the first truly cubist paintings...."[2]

Fernand Léger was also one of the founding fathers of Cubism. Léger, like Picasso and Braque, dismissed the painterly norms of the Renaissance and looked to the "so-called primitive epoch" for means to liberate painting from the servile copy of the subject."[3] Léger sought to portray natural forms through what he called "equivalents,"[4] or purified abstractions of the salient traits of the subject. Léger followed the Post-Impressionists in underplaying the subject and giving unequivocal emphasis to the basic structural properties of the object.

Analytic Cubism: 1906 to 1912–13

Analytic Cubism consisted of the paintings produced between 1906 and 1912 and was distinguished by the disintegration of objective form. The painters' disregard for realistic appearances grew out of their lack of interest in subject matter and preoccupation with subjective perception. Content and theme were no longer important considerations, and the Cubists painted subjects which would not provoke either emotional or intellectual associations in the viewer. Using mundane subjects, such as human figures, landscapes, and still-life, the Cubists dismantled the object and displaced the fragments in space so that the painted images were no longer representations of the subject but were independent visual images coexisting with the surroundings. The conflict between representation and structure resulted in the distortion of objective form.

In the Analytic phase, the Cubists were concerned with representing three-dimensional objects in a two-dimensional perspective and with the formal unity between foreground and background; their paintings, consequently, were distinguished by a shallow pictorial field. Their rationale for portraying a shallow landscape was that a three-dimensional perspective prevented the structural fusion of forms in the background with forms in the foreground. Accentuating the structural interaction of object and field, the Cubists abandoned recognizable shapes rendered in three-dimensionality but retained those aspects of three-dimensionality which could be carried over to a two-dimensional design. The Cubists produced a shallow pictorial field yet preserved the objective nature of space. The Cubists abandoned illusionism for geometric abstraction and worked, in the Analytic phase, toward "a language of pure structure,"[5] toward the abstraction and synthesis of form.

Picasso, in *The Reservoir, Horta de Ebro* (1909), and Braque, in *Le Port* (1909), reduced reality to underlying essential forms. The cityscape in Picasso's painting was depicted as an ascending mound of triangles, monoliths with flat and peaked tops, squares, cubes, and rectangles with strong, angular contour markings. Braque's boat was given a rectilinear hull, a cylindrical mast, and flat sheets for sails that merged into the severe geometric architecture of the landscape behind that faceted sea. The geometric forms in these paintings provided skeletal outlines of the subjects and created impressions of their actual appearances. The basis of the new Analytic Reality was the relationship between the subject and its underlying shape. Essential traits of the subject were no longer only "seen," but they became "the basis of the 'seen' form."[6]

Geometricization

Portraying objects in elemental shapes, the Cubist articulated a new reality: a world of geometrical construction. In the years between 1908 and 1912, Picasso and Braque developed the geometrical icons hinted at in their paintings of the previous two years. Subjects were depicted in massive solids, large, frontal, flattened planes and volumes. It was their preoccupation with geometricization, with "cubes," that gave the Cubist painters their name.*[7]

Braque's *Still-Life With Violin and Pitcher* (1909-10) contained diverse geometric shapes depicting the voluminous nature of the subject; these basic geometric forms split and opened at the edges, spilling over into the adjacent field. The picture surface appeared as a shallow terrain of rectangles, trapezoids, pyramids, curvilinear planes, small and large cubes, all broken at the seams, their geometric substance infusing other areas of the canvas. The underlying geometric forms of the pitcher and violin supplied Braque with a paradigm of shapes for articulating the massive abstract terrain. Braque sacrificed the identities of the subjects to the geometric rendering of the pictorial space.

In the Analytic phase, elemental geometric shapes supplied the Cubist painters with a "familial class of forms"[8] that they spread over the picture surface in an intricate system of interconnected planes to create an impression of volume. The continuous interaction of geometric forms, planes and volumes in space, the harmonious clash of surface and depth, produced a sensation of dynamism in the invented assemblage, and a new kind of compositional order.

Return to Architectonic Order

Picasso described Cubism as "the manifestation of a vague desire on the part of those of us who participated in it to get back to some kind of order...to move in a direction opposite to Impressionism...to search again for an architectonic basis in the composition...."[9] The architecture of the subject gave the Cubists a structural order, or a scheme, for building the picture. The escalating columns, rectangles, and planes in Picasso's *The Reservoir, Horta de Ebro* were distributed over the shallow, tilted picture surface in a synthesis of volumes. The fusion of these volumes was worked out of the underlying structure of the subject: the curvilinear wall of the reservoir, the rectangular shapes of the buildings and their reflections in the water. These forms were faceted in one architectural mass, which became the structural theme of the painting. Picasso created the architectonic pictorial content by abstracting and faceting the architecture of the subject; although the planes and volumes in Picasso's painting described real aspects of the subject, their primary function was to build the architectural order of the composition.

Open Planar Structure

Picasso's *The Reservoir* was a pivotal work in the transition from *closed* to *open* planar structure. The sides and tops of the buildings and columns were substantially closed and locked in space by bold, accentuated contour markings. The junctures between the frontal planes and volumes were delineated by rigid borders, preserving the autonomy of each plane and volume. Where the buildings encroached on one another, where the planes merged and intruded on one another, the definite contours prevented the shapes from merging with one another. The shapes were closed and immediately discernible because the underlying architectonic order of the subjects was not violated. The bases of some of these buildings, however, were left *open,* the bottom contours erased, and the planes that defined the buildings ran into the planes of the adjacent ground.

During the summer of 1910, Picasso and Braque tore into the contours of planes and volumes to create a network of transparent, overlapping planes that faded in and out of one another. Their intention was to eliminate the distortion of recognizable form that resulted from the close resemblance of the closed planar constructions to real objects. Picasso's *Portrait of Daniel-Henry Kahnweiler* (1910) was built of open-ended cubes and blocks running into one another without apparent logic. Some lines merged occasionally to complete a recognizable image, such as a wisp of hair, the nose and lip below, crossed hands, and a bottle and vase to the subject's right. A year later, Picasso painted *Still-Life With Clarinet* (1911), omitting realistic features and literal references to the subject; the painting consisted of an abstract assemblage of open, interlaced transparent planes. Through open planar structure, the Cubist painters preserved only the architectonic, anatomical structure of the subject to create either mere suggestions of objects and their spacial placement or highly abstract, nonrepresentational renderings.

Picasso and Braque eliminated verisimilitude through open planar structure and in the process created problems for themselves and the viewer. A complex pattern of overlapping, interlocking planes obscured not only the appearance of the subject but also the relationship among the new salient structural properties that they incorporated into the abstract picture. It became increasingly difficult for the viewer to recognize the subject and enter the picture plane. The exchange between foreground and background became increasingly diffuse, and the obliteration of recognizable shapes accelerated the disorientation brought on by abstraction.

The paintings produced before 1910 involved the viewer directly with the canvas. The scattered recognizable suggestions, or indices, of the subject provided hints or clues; the viewer was able to discern the parts, piece them together, and mentally reconstruct the subject. After 1910, recognition of the subject became more difficult as the composition became more abstract. Gleizes and Metzinger encouraged the Cubists to paint the world in an abstract conceptual mode but also warned them that "the reminiscence of natural forms cannot be absolutely banished...."[10]

Typographical Elements and Realistic Clues

Picasso and Braque became aware of the problems with abstraction and introduced undistorted realistic features of the depicted subjects as well as words, letters, and numbers in an effort to help the viewer locate the subject. Braque's *Still-Life With Violin and Pitcher* (1909–10) contained a realistically painted nail at the top of the abstract mass of planes and volumes; in *Still-Life With Fruit-Dish and Glass* (1912), Braque ran the word "BAR" off the upper right corner of the canvas and brought the word "ALE" into the lower left corner. In *Still-Life With Chair-Caning* (1912), Picasso painted an abbreviation, "JOU," for "Journal," the French word for newspaper.

The typographical and realistic clues were not superfluous inclusions. They functioned as specific referents to the subject of the painting and bridged the gap between abstraction and cognition. These inclusions provoke memory-images in the viewer, who pieces the realistic clues together with the abstract forms to construct the subject. In this way, the Cubists retained a reminiscence of the subject without sacrificing the conceptual portrayal. The paintings contained only the scheme of forms and small real details as stimuli integrated into the unity of the work so that "the finished product of the assimilation" existed in the mind of the viewer.[11]

Typographical elements not only described some feature of the subject, making cognition possible, but they also resembled the diagrammatic Cubist forms the painters used to depict the subject. Letters and words functioned as iconic analogues to the architectonic shapes in the painting and became integral pictorial elements of the Cubist design. Analyzing Braque's *Homage to J. S. Bach* (1912), Max Kozloff notices that the letters of the composer's name — painted boldly across the center of the canvas — were obvious repetitions of the "B," "H," and "S" patterns subtly worked throughout the painting. He goes on to explain that the "analogues between word and image" were not carried so far as to "sacrifice the decorative and contrast values of verbal symbols...within [the] pictorial atmosphere."[12] The letters were paradigmatic items of the familial forms used to compose the picture and, at the same time, functioned as an independent raised motif on the two-dimensional surface.

Perceptual Areas and Visual Gestalt

One of the devices the Cubists borrowed from Cézanne and went on to perfect was the division of the picture plane into independent perceptual areas that were ultimately bound by their participation in a visual gestalt. Cézanne depicted objects in moderate geometric shapes, constructing planes out of the geometry of the subject. Each geometric plane had its own nucleus, its own gravitational pull to a central point in its interior. This procedure, rendering independent perceptual areas with individual nuclei, opposed illusionistic procedures in which all forms were directed toward a single nucleus in the picture.

The Cubists elaborated Cézanne's practice so that eventually the dispersion of independent perceptual areas over the picture surface became idiosyncratic of Cubist painting. As early as 1907, Picasso distorted the figures in *Les Demoiselles* by rendering their anatomies in flat, schematic independent planes. The squatted figure, for example, appeared as a contorted assemblage of cylinders for leg and thigh, a broad flat tapering board for back and waist, and a primitive, voluminous mask for a face.

Picasso ignored the conventions of realistic human figure depiction and made the figure a conglomeration of geometric planes, each plane being a semi-autonomous construct. By 1913, every plane in the painting was a self-sufficient area, including the typographical elements and realistic clues, which had both autonomous thematic implications as well as autonomous structural properties.

Picasso composed *The Card Player* (1913–14) with numbers, letters, abstract geometric planes, fleurs-de-lis, moulding, and simulated wood-graining. The painting was divided into areas of specific reference that, when combined, contributed to the theme of the painting: a card player in a cafe. The logic of the painting emerged from the association of parts, their independent self-explanatory references joined to describe and place the subject within a recognizable thematic context. Planes, volumes, and literal elements preserved their perceptual and thematic individuality yet transcended their superficial compartmental ordering to participate in the structural continuum of the painting. Cubism invented a structural order in which it was possible to exaggerate pictorial forms and simultaneously transcend them. The independent perceptual areas were self-sufficient forms as well as integral components of the visual gestalt of the entire painting.

An Anti-Climactic Landscape

Employing open planar structure, making perceptual areas independent forms and integral components of a larger picture, the Cubists produced a highly integrated and homogenous picture surface; the painting became a synthesized landscape in which all parts had equal strength. The painters refused to treat the subject as foreground, to visually differentiate the subject from the background; rather, they preferred to fuse subject and field together in space. Picasso blended planes and volumes across the picture surface in an architectural unity; Braque resolved problems of contrasting volumes, shapes, and areas by giving all elements equal importance. Juan Gris referred to this integration as "a synthesis by the expression of the relationship between objects...."[13]

Picasso's *Ma Jolie* (1911) demonstrated the difference between the synthesis of parts in Cubism and the synthesis found in more traditional paintings. *Ma Jolie* was built as a vertical linear grid ruptured by strong diagonal vectors. The imagery consisted of a realistically drawn clef, an abstract but recognizable hand, the words "ma jolie," and the usual assortment of Cubistic geometric shapes. Where the imagery in a traditional painting was *placed* or *set* in a prefabricated, illusionistic context, the imagery in *Ma Jolie originated in and precipitated* pictorial space. The space contained the image, and the image contained the space; image and space were firmly united in a shallow field. The imagery was not set against the field but interacted with it so that foreground and background participated equally as structural components in the continuum of the picture plane.

The landscape effect in Cubist painting evolved from Cézannian "passage," in which foreground and background were joined by condensing the structural features of the subject and the field. Picasso and Braque, after 1910, closed the three-dimensional space by bringing the background forward, welding the figure and its surroundings. The synthesis of figure and field on a two-dimensional surface prompted William Barrett to call Cubism an "anticlimactic" art. Unlike art with "pictorial climax," where the central figure dominated the field, Cubism emphasized both the "negative spaces" and the "positive spaces," making the picture space a continuum of equal parts.[14] The surface of the Cubist painting was both the source and the conclusion of all the pictorial elements because the surface represented the totality of the painting.

The shallow landscape of Cubism directed the viewer through the incessant dialogue between surface and depth. Looking at Picasso's *Bottle and Glass* (1911), John Berger notices that the eye started at the surface, followed the forms into the picture plane, then out to the surface again, bringing an informed perception to the second observation of the surface:

> We begin with the surface, but since everything in the picture refers back to the surface we begin with the conclusion. We then search...for some understanding of the configuration of events whose interaction is the conclusion from which we began.... What we in fact do is to find the sign for what we have just discovered: a sign which was always there but which previously we could not read.[15]

Cubism projected a new mode of perceiving the world. It was not a metaphor for abstraction but for a new vision, "a new reality."[16]

Synthetic Cubism: 1912–1913 on

Collage and Papier-collé

The Cubists, in the Synthetic period, created sculpted, highly textured surfaces. They continued to reduce abstraction through typographical inclusions and literal referents and added textural characteristics of the depicted subjects. *Collage* first appeared in Braque's *Still-Life With Fruit-Dish and Glass* (1912), when strips of wood-grained wallpaper were glued on the canvas to indicate a drawer and table top. Pasting strips of paper and other found materials on the picture surface, the Cubists invented a means of describing objects and increasing the textural value of the painting.

Collage was the use of natural materials, such as sand, displaced manufactured objects, such as tickets, programs, wallpaper, and cardboard, and any other materials foreign to a painterly or pictorial context. The Cubists employed actual or fabricated surfaces of an object as signs to refer to, but not to imitate, the actual physical appearance of the subject. In *Still-Life With Chair-Caning,* Picasso applied caning to portray a chair; Braque used corrugated cardboard to indicate a musical staff and the sound of a clarinet in *Musical Instruments* (1918). The real objects were facsimiles of the literal, textural and aural aspects of the subjects and became not only art materials but also the subject of the paintings; the means of composition provided the motif.

Collage enabled the painters to present spatial relations directly either by overlapping several strips of material or by juxtaposing painted lines with the contours of the found materials. Areas on the flattened picture plane were defined in front of and behind strips of material, the strips functioning as partitions on the picture surface. The picture plane was divided into many separate areas by the junctures of overlapping and intersecting continuous lines as the Cubists continued, in the Synthetic phase, to disregard illusionistic devices.

A Plastic Consciousness: Subject-as-Object,
Object-as-Plastic Sculpture

It was the means of painting that interested the Cubists, not rendering an accurate or realistic portrayal of the subject. In the process, subject matter became irrelevant, was neutralized, and was finally treated simply as an object on which to try new means of composition. Whether a landscape, an interior scene, or a portrait, the subject was given the same objective treatment as the space around it.

Perfected in the Synthetic phase, the objective treatment of the subject actually first appeared in rudimentary form in *Les Demoiselles,* when Picasso used the sharp, angular and planar shapes found in Ivory Coast masks to portray both a bowl of fruit and the crouching figure. This was an effort on Picasso's part to produce a "plastic effect" in the painting.[17] It was what Gleizes and Metzinger called "the integration of the plastic consciousness"[18] that drove the Cubists to dissociate the subject from its normal appearance and context and to exploit its objective presence as a part of the formal environs.

The Cubist norm was to proportion objects according to their plastic geometric potential. They believed the object-as-form had an absolute value in itself, and this value could best be realized by overstating its plasticity. Picasso and Braque used simple geometric shapes to enhance the plasticity of the object, rendering the subject in cylinders, rectangles, cubes, volumes, and planes. Their intention was to *sculpt* geometric, plastic icons and preserve a feeling of three-dimensionality and depth in the shallow field.

Analytic Cubism created an impression of sculpture through closed planar construction, but when the strong, sharp contours began to open and intermingle, the "sculptural illusion" became obscured. The Cubists regained the sculptural illusion in Synthetic Cubism by making their painted forms press outward from pictorial depth into the viewer's space, and, in this way, they achieved "an increase in sculptural presence."[19]

The outward thrust of the pictorial plane was achieved by curtailing the surface/depth dialogue between foreground and background. While contours of forms and areas were inextricably blended in the later stages of Analytic Cubism, the sculpted forms and areas of Synthetic Cubism were closed by either real or implied boundaries, and the distance between objects and masses became noticeable; as the separation between forms became more noticeable, the content of the painting became more comprehensible.

Condensed Signs

Although their Synthetic works grew more comprehensible, Picasso and Braque continued to produce abstract compositions. The painted or sculpted icon still presented only an impression of the subject. Using found materials, typographical clues, and texture, the Cubists created *signs* to indicate particular aspects of the subject: a pipe, fruit, titles of periodicals, buttons, dice, simulated wood-graining and hair. The Cubists treated pictorial forms as *condensed signs* that contained a synthesis of the chief attributes of the subject or theme. *The Three Musicians* (1922) consisted of flattened, sculpted plastic forms that were abstract, but precise, signs of the depicted objects. Rectangles and musical notations represented score sheets, a cylinder with a black circle at its base a clarinet, and overlapped spheres a guitar.

The condensed sign was a fusion of form and content. It created itself as an object, as an independent form, even though it contained a sense of the depicted subject. The condensed signs in *The Three Musicians* projected references to real objects but were also self-sufficient forms creating an abstract thematic context. The cylinder and black circle suggested a clarinet on one level, but on another, more abstract plane they were simply two forms joined in space: a cylinder terminating in a black circle. In this painting, the content was the form, and the form embraced the content.

The Fourth Dimension and Pictorial Structure

Jean Metzinger believed that if Cubism was fully to achieve the ends toward which it aspired, it would have to invent a dimension beyond the third. The third dimension satisfactorily presented the object at a given moment but inadequately expressed "a synthesis of views and feelings toward the object."[20] The Cubists reacted against the limitations of the third dimension by exploring "new possibilities of spatial measurement which...[were] designated by the term: the fourth dimension."[21]

The fourth dimension, according to Apollinaire, originated in the three dimensions of Euclidean geometry and represented "the immensity of space eternalyzing itself in all directions at any given moment."[22] The fourth dimension presented the object in time and in several directions simultaneously and, in this way, expressed spatial relationships directly, giving the object in space its maximum plasticity.

Paul Laporte, in an article "Cubism and Science," writes that the theories of Cubism and physics were analogous because each dealt with the nature of space and time simultaneously.[23] He describes the fourth dimension as a space-time continuum in which the components were not regarded as absolutes "but must be considered as being in an integral and functional relationship with one another."[24] Participating in one functional relationship, space and time were to be treated as equal parts in one continuum.

The four-dimensional space-time continuum was used to explain the integration of the visual experience with the kinesthetic experience in Cubism. The Cubists dismantled and distorted the object in an effort to achieve new means of objective portrayal; by fracturing the object, they forced the viewer to scan the painting for structural aspects of the subject, then to assemble these parts as the eye moved over the canvas. The continuity of the subject emerged through the movement of the eyes, through the continuity of memory. To fuse many aspects of the subject simultaneously in one image was to reproduce the movement of the eye in time and through space, and consequently to reconstitute the subject in time. Unlike the Futurists, who portrayed movement as a series of still figures, the Cubists transformed the "dynamics of perception into the physically static medium of two-dimensional painting."[25] In this way, the Cubists gave the pictorial space a dynamic quality analogous to kinesthetic experience. The integration of the visual with the kinesthetic experience could only be achieved by dismissing illusionistic treatments and reconstructing the object in a spatial, formal, and temporal cohesion.

Parts of objects were not to be treated in isolation but in their functional relationships with one another in space and time. The length of the object was considered not as a fact of the object but as a relationship between the object and the viewer; the same consideration was applied to time and mass. The object transcended its locality, its status as a "point in time" placed in space, to become "an event in time" manifested in "finite space"; the object was considered an *event* in a perceptual field.[26]

The "event quality" could only be expressed by breaking up the formal and local properties of the object as it was seen by one viewer from one fixed viewpoint. Portraying objects in their most elemental geometric features, integrating surface and depth on a two-dimensional plane, giving space the formal characteristics of the objects that filled it, and fusing several successive appearances of the subject in one image, the Cubists incorporated the kinesthetic experience in their pictorial representations.

Pictorial space in Cubism was enhanced because it became not a mere container for events but "part of the continuity of the events within it."[27] Cubism built "a sensitive calligraphy" that synthesized conflicting elements into a unity of relations and interactions. Cubism constituted a *pictorial fact,* pushing the balance between representation and pictorial structure in the direction of structure. The objective of Cubism was to create a highly integrated system of pictorial events through familial forms in pictorial space; this goal was realized in "a pictorially consistent structure,"[28] in a four-dimensional landscape.

Movement in Cubist Painting

Laporte attributes pictorial innovations in Cubism to the space-time continuum of the fourth dimension.[29] His opinion is based on his understanding of simultaneity in Cubist painting. It was the relative natures of space and time in a closed continuum that enabled Picasso to render several separate aspects of an object in one image. Picasso transformed the "dynamism of perception into the physically static medium"[30] of Cubism and added implications of passing time and motion to the picture plane.

The Post-Impressionists precipitated the practice of giving motion to static entities. They depicted reality as rhythmical sequences of geometric shapes connected in space. The Cubists embellished this technique in the "clockwork mechanism" of their abstract, architectonic constructions.[31] They infused their paintings with great amounts of mechanized energy by exaggerating the staccato rhythm in the interaction of architectural forms; the abrupt spacial divisions between objects and masses in Synthetic Cubism produced an equally abrupt rhythm across the picture plane.

Dynamism in Léger's constructions appeared in strong, sinuous rhythmic patterns. Painting small disjointed images in rapid succession, Picasso modeled the interaction of shapes in his work after the movement of the human body and the stroboscopic effect. Picasso, in *Seated Woman* (1926–27) fractured the pictorial image, only to reassemble the parts in rhythmically superimposed planes; in his double-face heads of 1937 and 1939, he produced a kinesthetic sensation, using spatial recessions and protrusions to fuse the central image. Movement in these works evolved from the sequence of juxtaposed flat surfaces and contrasting volumes.

Although Picasso produced these works several years after Futurist experiments with movement, they exhibited no substantial likeness to Futurist creations. The dynamism in Picasso's work was achieved as it was in his earlier works: by transforming "the kinesthetic experience of three-dimensional space. . .into purely visual elements."[32]

The sensation of motion in Cubism was achieved by depicting the subject as an "inorganic assembly of parts—mere anatomical signs. . .;"[33] this "machine metaphor" is described as cinematographic movement by Standish Lawder in *The Cubist Cinema.* Lawder believes that the Cubists' portrayal of motion was shaped by the writings of Henry Bergson, whose theories of "fluid time" and "cinematographical" perception reduced form and motion to "a snapshot view of a transition."[34] What Bergson saw as cinematographic image—a fusion of several viewpoints presented simultaneously in patterns of form and light—bore a close resemblance to simultaneity and kinesthetic sensation in Cubist painting.[35]

Lawder also attributes expressions of motion in Cubism to the physiologist Jules-Etienne Marey.[36] Using a photographic gun, a forerunner to the motion picture camera, Marey produced chronophotographs in which human and animal locomotion was exhibited as a series of simultaneous images inextricably united in space and time.

The most striking correlation between movement in Cubist painting and movement in cinematography appeared in the experiments of the Cubist painter Leopold Survage. Survage started a project in 1912, called *Le Rhythme Coloré,* in which he intended to use colored geometric forms in motion to produce "a rhythm of melodic and harmonic relationships moving through time."[37] The project was interrupted by the First World War, but Survage managed to complete several drawings for his film. In the extant portions of *Le Rhythme Coloré,* the movement of the colored shapes resembled the rhythmic interplay of shapes in Cubist paintings: the movement of shapes toward and away from the camera corresponded to the continuous exchange between foreground and background; the film projected the same sensation of kinesthetic activity as a Cubist painting; and dismantled forms were integrated in melodic, plastic transfiguration.

Gleizes and Metzinger wrote in *Du Cubisme* that the rhythmic interaction of shapes in Cubist painting produced a "dynamism of form."[38] Their position was modified and developed by more recent historians, who contended that not only were forms mobilized, but they were activated according to the principles of kinesthesia. Kinesthesia, in Bergson's analysis, was like the "mechanism of our ordinary knowledge," being of a cinematographical kind...."[39]

Color and Light

Contributing to the shallow, anticlimactic impressions of Cubist paintings was the unusual handling of chiaroscuro and color in both Analytic and Synthetic Cubism. In the earlier phase, the painters used monochromatic colors to accentuate the impression of depth created by tonal contrasts. In addition, the light and dark contrasts enhanced the schematized picture by highlighting the many well-defined facets. Chiaroscuro reinforced the hard-edge contours of the bold geometric forms, and, at the same time, compressed the many facets and lines into the dense, light and dark speckled landscape. Shading in Analytic Cubism tilted the escalating planes into the shallow depth of the field.

When the Cubists added delicate color contrasts in the Synthetic phase, they were careful not to let color distract from the formal construction, the sculptural presence, of the paintings. The blues, pinks, greens, and ochers coded the various tectonic shapes, maintaining the individuality and solidity of each plane and volume in the picture. The Cubists also employed color to differentiate areas that overlapped, enhancing the sculpted appearance of shapes and areas.

Given the profuse pattern of light and dark contrasts over the picture surface and the many facets, each having its own nucleus, light in Cubist painting functioned to accentuate the many planes, volumes, and areas. When Picasso and Braque abandoned illusionistic techniques and one-point perspective, they no longer felt compelled to render light realistically. It could not be said that light came from any one direction because Picasso and Braque used light as a means to create form. The abstract, architectonic construction of the portrayal determined the pattern of illumination, and it was common for Cubist paintings to have many "hot" points across the surface; in this way, the paintings acquired several nuclei as opposed to one nucleus, and illumination became a means to further schematize the image.

2

Victory Over the Sun (1913)

Historian Peter Lufft wrote, in a monograph on "Kasimir Malevich Designs *Victory Over the Sun,*" that the "world's first Cubist theatrical spectacle" took place at St. Petersburg in 1913, in the form of a Futurist opera, *Victory Over the Sun.*[1] A monumental production in the history of the Russian avant-garde, *Victory Over the Sun,* with its radical staging, music, and literature, was primarily the work of composer Mikhail Matyushin, playwright Alexei Kruchenykh, and the artist Kasimir Malevich. Two other painters, Tilonov and Shkolnik, participated in the production rehearsals, but Malevich has been credited with the designs for scenery and costumes.

Matyushin explains that *Victory Over the Sun* embodied the reaction of his colleagues to "gradually rising changes in life and also...in creative work," particularly Impressionism, Cubism and Futurism.[2] Matyushin and his friends ridiculed bourgeois aesthetics in their garish parades, balls, raucous performances, and readings of alogical poetry at the Cafe Pittoresque in Moscow. Kruchenykh's opera reflected the rebellious spirit of the Russian youth; it was the story of modern man's search for an alternative to traditional world order and communication. Kruchenykh's heroes attacked the sun—symbol of artistic convention and archaic morality—tore it from the sky, and transformed world order and civility into bedlam. They replaced the old world order with a new aesthetics in which dissonance replaced harmony, alogicality and absurdity replaced reason, and language became a cacophony of nonsensical sound.

Produced at the Luna Park Theatre in December 1913, *Victory Over the Sun* was the product of a partnership between Cubo-Futurist poets and painters. Part of a symposium that included more than forty speeches, debates, and meetings, *Victory Over the Sun* was staged on consecutive evenings with Vladimir Mayakovsky's *Vladimir Mayakovsky: A Tragedy* after only two rehearsals.

The production demonstrated the new aesthetics of *Cubo-Futurism.* The term Cubo-Futurism was applied to the post-primitivist movement in Russian art and literature during the years 1911 and 1914. Cubo-Futurist works exhibited doctrinal and stylistic affinities with contemporary Western European movements, such as Cubism and Italian Futurism yet "was peculiar to Russia and immediately preceded the schools of abstract painting which arose in Russia during the years 1911–21, in which the Russians emerged at last as pioneers in the 'modern movement.'"[3] Visual artists such as Larionov, Goncharova, and Malevich disregarded the rules of painterly academicism, preferring to dissect and scatter painted objects over the picture surface, displace planes and spatial relationships, and invent forms through abstraction; musicians applied a similar radicalism, creating new pitches, dissonant melodies, a chorus of independent, simultaneous voices; writers dissociated words from meaning in order to invent a language of pure sound. These innovations of the Cubo-Futurist aesthetic culminated in *Victory Over the Sun.*

Despite the radical nature of the opera, the producers were criticized for actualizing only a small part of their revolutionary aesthetics: The libretto was incomplete and, except for a few transrational passages, had a logical informational construction; the orchestra consisted of only one out-of-tune piano; Matyushin used a fairly conventional musical structure to compose the score; and the performers were—apart from a few professional singers—students and amateurs who had been rejected by Maya-kovsky as performers in his play.

The historical importance of Kruchenykh's opera has been attributed primarily to the Cubist costumes and decor by Malevich.[4] Malevich and many other Russian artists at that time were largely influenced by Impressionism, Fauvism, and Cubism. Gleizes' and Metzinger's *Du Cubisme* was translated into Russian one year after its publication in France and became, in addition to the writings and reproductions of Cézanne, a popular resource among Russian artists between 1910 and 1914. Fernand Léger gained a sizable following in Russia, and it is likely that Malevich was inspired by reproductions, exhibitions, and reviews of Léger's work. Many paintings by Malevich bore stylistic similarities to Léger's paintings, including cubic division of the pictorial space and dense cylindrical forms in nonobjective representation.

Malevich, like his Cubist counterparts, used Cézanne's paintings as models for pictorial construction. The arrangement of the three figures in Malevich's *Chiropodist in the Bathroom* (1908–1909) seemed to be a copy of the arrangement of the figures in Cézanne's *The Card Players* (1890–92), a reproduction of which Malevich affixed to his wall.[5] Malevich rendered the pictorial surface of *Taking in the Harvest* (1911) in Cézannian cubes, cylinders, and spheres and combined abstract forms, angular and tubular figures, and mechanical rhythms in a flattened portrayal of interweaving planes. He eventually surpassed Cézanne and his Cubist mentors in his "logical approach toward abstract picture-construction"[6], but, by 1911, he had completely embraced a Cubist style and voiced a doctrinal affiliation with the Cubists on the back of his painting, *The Violin and the Cow* (1911): the picture represented "the alogical collusion of two forms,...the moment of struggle between logic, the natural law and bourgeois sense and prejudice."[7]

The Woodcutter (1911) was Malevich's first fully realized Cubo-Futurist painting. The Cubist element was particularly evident in the merger of figure and background into a simple, dynamic pattern of cylindrical forms and in the large, spacious frontal masses with heavy contour markings. Malevich continued to paint partly in a Cubist vein over the next several years; he used Picasso's *Musical Instruments* (1912–13) as a model for the Cubist works he painted late in 1913, just prior to his first Suprematist composition.

The origin of Suprematism lay in a design Malevich made for one of the backcloths in *Victory Over the Sun*. Most of the designs for this production consisted of basic geometric forms that resembled primitive icons and symbols. Malevich believed that basic geometric forms were the only appropriate forms for expressing what he thought to be the only legitimate concern of modern art: the realm of feelings as opposed to objects in reality.

Although the Expressionists embraced the same objective, Malevich employed extremely simplified, singular nonobjective forms – parallelograms and squares – or combinations of geometric forms in his early Suprematist paintings to create a purely nonrepresentational art; unlike those by Expressionists, Malevich's compositions did not resemble real objects; in their austere abstraction, his paintings seemed formalistically connected to Cubism or, at least, to Cubist geometricization as it appeared in his designs for *Victory Over the Sun.*

Like other artists who designed for Russian avant-garde productions, Malevich looked on stage design as something greater than mere pictorial ornamentation.[8] The stage space was a pictorial space, and Russian artists brought to their designs the radical appearances of modern art. Malevich's curtains, scenery, costumes, and backdrops resembled his Cubist paintings of the period and have been described as "unequivocally Cubist with strong Suprematist elements."[9]

The front curtain, which was apparently the first of two curtains used to open the opera, was a mixed-media design that prefigured the style of sets and costumes. The design consisted of overlapping, contoured squares, rectangles, truncated circles and ellipses, displaced axes, primitivist hieroglyphic figures, stylized distortions of anatomical appendages such as a hand and a foot, typographical letters, scribbled notes and letters. Stacked one on top of another, the shapes and forms created a two-dimensional abstract composition similar to Synthetic Cubist paintings. Malevich generously incorporated these Cubist elements into the scenery and stage effects.

How the opera began is unclear; that is, how the front curtain was "raised" to reveal a second. Malevich and Matyushin said, in an interview with a reporter from the newspaper *Den,* that "the curtain flew up, and the spectator found himself in front of a second one of white calico...."[10] Kolia Tomashevsky, an actor in the production, gave a different version. He reported that two Futurecountrymen delivered a short, quizzical prologue,[11] then "tore a paper curtain that was painted completely in Cubist style and the opera began."[12] (It seems reasonable to assume that the first curtain was painted, and the second was not. Had the second curtain been painted, it would have been a time-consuming chore to repaint it after it had been torn.)

Assuming that the Futurecountrymen tore the second curtain, a third curtain appeared before the audience. It is unclear from extant reports what design Malevich painted on this curtain. One report maintained that Kruchenykh, Matyushin, and Malevich were represented in "three different sets of hieroglyphics."[13] It is not certain whether the "sets of hieroglyphics" were visual depictions of the three men or hieroglyphic writing. In either case, if the hieroglyphic pictures were sketched in the same way as the figurines on the front curtain, then they would have resembled primitivist, grotesque geometrical constructions, like the figures in Picasso's *Dancers* (1907) or Braque's *Nude* (1908). The subjects in these two paintings were portrayed in bold, voluminous outlines poised in expressive gestures. Another account maintained that, after the prologue, a bright, colorful cardboard placard was lowered from the flies; this placard contained a painting of two warriors bathed in a blood red color.[14]

The third curtain split when the music began and revealed a simple, nonobjective painting on a backdrop.[15] It was this painting that supposedly precipitated Suprematism. Malevich painted a black and white square on the backcloth; a diagonal passing through the square from lower left to upper right separated the black area from the white. This backdrop was one of several against which the action was played and was probably the most simply conceived.

Rainer Crone, writing in *Art Forum* (December 1978), suggests that the sketch of this backcloth was *not* the first instance of Suprematism but was the representation of a part of the circumference of the sun set against a black universe. The reasoning behind this suggestion is that the line separating the dark and light areas did not make a perfect diagonal; instead, it was a slightly curved line that touched the base line of the square, forming only one white triangle. This triangle is thought to represent the sun. If it was a representational sketch, it was not nonobjective and could not have been a Suprematist composition.

Crone believes that it was another sketch for this production that actually precipitated the nonobjective formalism of Suprematism. This design contained several parallelograms and trapezoids arranged in a two-dimensional, nonillusionistic, and totally abstract manner. In any event, both sources attributed the origin of Suprematism to the Cubist-inspired designs for *Victory Over the Sun.*

The backcloths of Act I, Scene II, and Act II, Scenes V and VI, were typical examples of Malevich's Cubist scenery. Kruchenykh's stage directions for Act I, Scene II, called for green walls and floor to depict a world without flowers.[16] The semi-objective, two-dimensional design consisted primarily of large rectilinear blocks for walls, ceiling, and floor; these were displayed simultaneously on the single plane of the backcloth. The floor and right wall were divided by color into irregular, independent, and contrasting squares and rectangles; the color demarcations on the ceiling created overlapping triangles and several low rectangles, perhaps to represent a roof, all placed on top of the square that made up the back wall.

A spiral dominated the rear panel, and three other forms resembling musical notations were placed to the side of the spiraling curve. The spiral, reversed musical notes on the rear panel, and three half-note marks on the ceiling appeared as typographical or realistic elements: recognizable shapes providing literal references in an assemblage of rectilinear, abstract forms. A wheel protruded from the bottom right corner of the square of the back panel, its circumference marked by a thick, light-colored curving band, its interior darkened and supporting a light-colored figure like the hieroglyphs on the front curtain.

Malevich painted a totemic construction on the left wall; this totem consisted of two diffuse and transparent rectangles piled one on top of the other with the bottom rectangle balanced on the apex of a triangle. The remaining shapes on the backcloth were geometric and nonobjective and were illuminated by a light that seemed to emanate from the interior of the painted surface in the same way that light emanated from within Cubist paintings.

The backcloth for Act II, Scenes V and VI, depicted the "Tenth Country" and was a more complex, but comprehensible, Cubist construction. The stage directions for Scene V described the Tenth Country as exterior walls of houses with windows that "go toward the inside in a strange way as if they are pipes drilled through walls. Many windows, placed in irregular rows and they seem to be moving in a suspicious way."[17] The description for Scene VI also referred to the house that was "fenced in."[18]

This backdrop displayed strong Cubist elements. The house was depicted in a flattened hierarchy of squares and rectangles which represented walls, roof, and partitions. Cylinders represented chimneys and spirals staircases. Linear grids stood for ladders and windows. Circles were a clock, the sun, and perhaps a porthole in the roof. Rendered in severe architectonic forms, the painting employed simultaneity, since the front, sides, and roof were combined in a single, two-dimensional edifice.

Malevich distorted perspective by painting nonreferential geometric shapes on the two-dimensional shell of the building. An inverted "L" scaled the wall, and other ambiguous shapes protruded from either side. Four triangles anchored to a curving line at the bottom of the backcloth could have been construed as a fence or as additional geometric forms painted on the picture plane to deform the subject and heighten the two-dimensional feeling. Light was handled in this design as in the previous one: without regard to realistic or illusionistic effect.

A photograph from the production pictured Kruchenykh lying across the laps of Malevich and Matyushin, who were seated in front of a backdrop of randomly placed, inverted drop and wings. It is not known whether this setting was used in the actual performance, although a stage direction in Scene VI read: "the Fat Man peeps inside the watch: the tower the sky the streets are upside down — as in a mirror."[19] If this background was used during the performances, it represented an infinitely subtle application of Cubist aesthetics: a first-order duplex structure in which the unmatched drop and wings acted as a *message* of Cubist perception. The diverse icons turned upside down became pure forms, fractured, dispersed, and abstract in the invented assemblage. Overlapping the *message* function, the drop and wings operated as a *code* for Cubist collage. The flats provided suggestions of location and function, as well as texture, and acted as a background for various icons (the costumed performers), all of which were literal in their identities (as characters) and at the same time nonreferential as components in an abstract configuration.

Malevich's Cubist scenery, the twenty large pieces of decor which he built in only four days, was exactly what Kruchenykh had envisaged for the production. Writing in his memoirs, Kruchenykh mentioned that he believed a Cubist pictorial vocabulary should dominate the designs for *Victory Over the Sun:* "The scenery and stage effects were as I expected and wanted.... The scenery by Malevich was made of big sheets — triangles, circles, bits of machinery."[20] The picture plane framed by the proscenium was rendered in geometric forms, displaced perceptual axes, disjointed perspectives, two-dimensional portrayals on flat, frontal surfaces, and abstract architectonic assemblages. Malevich employed "...the whole rich world of Cubism with its...many figurative and abstract signs, letters and inscriptions, details from the world of technology...projectiles, segments of a circle, numbers and objects from both cosmic and terrestrial realms."[21]

Malevich's designs for the costumes resembled his designs for the scenery. Constructed of cardboard, wire, and papier-mâché, the costumes were conceived as extensions of Cubist figure portrayals with their flattened and architectonic features. The performers wore papier-mâché head masks and body masks, the former measuring approximately half the height of the actor's bodies. Kruchenykh described the masks as "modern gasmasks" and referred to the actors as "moving machines" with "marionette gestures."[22]

The costume for the Futurecountry Strongman consisted of a number of cones and triangles fused into an architectonic figure. The shoulders were built of an upright isosceles triangle, the breast plate an inverted triangle, and the waist and hips an upright irregular triangle. Triangles and cones hooked at the joints represented arms and legs, and a cone with a rounded top made up the head.

These parts created a visual interplay of stacked planes and volumes that described the character; fashioned in geometric shapes, the figure resembled the stacked architectonic composition in Braque's *Houses at L'Estaque* and Picasso's *The Reservoir, Horta de Ebro*. The Cubists' paintings and Malevich's Futurecountry Strongman were reduced to essential geometric shapes; these shapes were then mounted one on top of the other so that the contour markings were linear, angular, and pronounced. The identity of Malevich's character, like the subjects in early Cubist paintings, emerged from the architectural construction.

Malevich's design for A Coward had a similar construction. Whereas the Futurecountry Strongman consisted of an interplay of volumes and planes, the Coward consisted of planes only. The arms and legs were long rectangles, the torso was a sculptured triangular bodice, and the head a rigid, two-dimensional, triangular mask topped by a square hat with a long linear brim. The costume for the Coward, like Picasso's painting *Female Nude* (1910), was made of planes fused at the edges to represent the junctions of the parts of the body. The Coward and *Female Nude* were rendered to project primarily a sensation of planar formalism.

Malevich's other costume and mask designs approximated Cubist styles, particularly the mask for the New Man, which bore a strong likeness to the face of the stooped woman in *Les Demoiselles*. The heads of both subjects were realized in angular, flattened primitive designs with shadows on the left side producing an impression of volume.

Simultaneity was given a unique treatment in Kruchenykh's text, where Nero and Caligula appeared "combined in one person."[23] Malevich did not portray two identities in one body but represented the dual-identities in two contrasting colors.

Crone remarks that Malevich's "stylistic origin and obligation" lay in early Analytic Cubism:

...feet, arms and individual parts of the body were already conceived as somewhat flat surfaces to a similar degree by Picasso around 1908, and even the unity of the figure itself, despite the more drastic geometrical reduction by Malevich, is comparable to Picasso.[24]

Cubist Lighting

An innovative lighting technique, also designed by Malevich, emphasized the Cubistic features of the costumes and set pieces. Peter Lufft described the lighting as "pure Cubism."[25] Light was not used simply to illuminate the stage or to create an atmosphere, nor was it employed to reproduce naturalistic illumination. Malevich applied the lighting schemes of the Post-Impressionists and Cubists. Light was used to accentuate form, to sculpt objects in space.

Kruchenykh recalled a "blinding light from the projectors,"[26] and Peter Lufft described "the harsh light of glaring projectors" illuminating only parts of objects.[27] Using light as a scalpel, Malevich dissected the objects and actors on stage in the way the Cubists dissected their subjects; only the essential features were highlighted. Beams of light picked out conical heads, cylindrical trunks and appendages, dispersing fragments of geometric bodies over the stage space. Given the geometric and architectonic features of the costumes and scenery, Malevich's lighting scheme produced an abstract composition of sculpted, geometric masses. The result was a stage picture that resembled either Analytic Cubism or Cubist collage.

Reconstructing Act II, Scene V, it is possible to recreate the Cubist effect in the mixture of background, costumes, and selective lighting. Scene V took place in the Tenth Country and was performed in front of the backdrop with the Cubistically rendered house described above. A New Man entered at one side of the stage, a Coward at the other side, the characters speaking alternately.

The bright beams of light lit parts of the architectonic costumes—the large rectilinear torso of the Coward or the inverted cones at the cuffs of the New Man—and highlighted these fragments against the architectonic construction on the backdrop. The result was a flattened, formalistic fusion of foreground and background. The Coward's triangular torso appeared as a large planar form, as a mass or volume with a formal affinity to the shaded triangular planes on the siding of the house. The triangular torso also described the subject, the Coward, and, in this way, functioned as a condensed sign of the character. The same treatment was given to the New Man, with its conical cuffs and flattened chest shield of trapezoids. When the beams of light struck the shield, with its light and dark contrast and the character's thighs—the left a voluminous hemisphere and the right a tapering trapezoid—these parts blended perfectly with the light and dark contrasts in the backdrop and with the diverse architectural features of the house.

When the two costumes were illuminated simultaneously and separated in space with the backcloth between them, the stage picture contained various geometric forms dispersed through space; these forms were integrated by the architectonic matrix on the backdrop. The individual identities of the characters were subordinated to the scheme of geometric shapes; the illuminated fragments of the costumes were visually linked with parts of the background, forming areas of related and identical shapes. The stage picture consisted of a synthesized, shallow dialogue between foreground and background, between surface and depth.

Reviewing both Kruchenykh's and Lufft's descriptions of the production, it seemed reasonable to question the exactitude with which the "blinding light" and "harsh light of glaring projectors" was able to pick out the individual features of the costumes without spilling into other areas. The clearest account of the precision of Malevich's lighting scheme was that of the Futurist writer, Benedict Livshitz:

> From this night of the first-born the feelers of the projectors picked out parts now of this, now of that object and imbued it with life by saturating it with light...The figures themselves were cut into shape with the knives of the searchlights and robbed alternately of their arms, legs, or head, since for Malevich they were only geometrical bodies subject not merely to dissection into their component parts but also to complete extinction within the picture space. The only reality was the abstract form that absorbed the whole Luciferian haste of the world.[28]

Here Livshitz states not only that the lights were wholly successful in isolating certain parts of the costumes but also that the lighting integrated all aspects of the scenic ensemble in a landscape of familial forms. Of particular interest in his account were the phrases "geometrical bodies subject...to complete extinction within the picture space," and "the only reality was the abstract form that absorbed the whole...." These descriptions verify the suspicion that, given the Cubist treatment of decor and costumes, the narrow playing area that, according to Crone, measured ten feet by eight feet, and the dissected "geometrical bodies" standing close to the geometrical backcloths, Rappaport and Malevich created a stage picture strikingly similar to the homogenous landscape in Cubist paintings.

Cubist Language

Cubo-Futurist poets, such as Kruchenykh and Khlebnikov, invented a transrational language known as *Zaum*. Zaum was a hybrid construction of Cubistic and Futuristic elements and formed what Rainer Crone calls "the cornerstone of a cubo-futuristic 'esthetic'."[29] It is possible to disentangle the two disciplines and analyze the specific contributions of each to this transrational language and this new hybrid aesthetics. Looking closely at the way Kruchenykh employed the Zaum-language in *Victory Over the Sun*, particularly as it was manifested in performance, it becomes apparent that Cubism supplied the Russian poets with an underlying structure, or a means, for constructing a Cubo-Futurist speech.

The Cubo-Futurist poets fabricated a new radical poetry by replacing conventional language with an invented phonetics; ephithets, colloquialisms, nonsensical words, gibberish, and infantile language were combined with the new rules of grammar and syntax. Words were broken, rejoined in illogical and esoteric combinations, and placed in a transrational context with neologisms and pure sound. Kruchenykh transferred these experiments in poetry to the dialogue in *Victory Over the Sun*. Tomashevsky recalled the characters speaking and singing "unmitigated nonsense and nothing else."[30]

Kruchenykh irritated the director, Rappaport, by frequently interrupting rehearsals and directing the performers to pronounce words and sounds with pauses in between; in this way, Kruchenykh dissected the dialogue into planes and patterns of sound so that at points it was punctuated by silences: "The cam-el-like fac-to-ries al-read-y threat-en us. . . ."[31] Most of the libretto was spoken, there being only two singing parts. What lyrics were sung consisted entirely of vowels for the songs of the Coward and of consonants for the songs of the Aviator; these were sung dissonantly with frequent intervals between syllables and words. These devices had the effect of separating words and lyrics from meaning while accentuating the sonorous substance of speech.

Kruchenykh's experiments with the sonorous construction of dialogue and lyrics resembled the Cubists' experiments in pictorial imagery. Fracturing the subject, recomposing it in an invented and stylized pictorial language, the Cubists alienated visual form from meaning, substance from expression. Kruchenykh likewise separated substance and expression, preferring to subordinate the meanings of words to their sounds.

Words and lyrics, like Cubist pictorial forms, were arranged in an intricate pattern of familial forms. Where the Cubists expressed the structure of real objects in underlying geometric forms, Kruchenykh expressed the structure of speech in its most basic structural unit: vowels and consonants. Where the Cubists described their subjects in dispersed familial shapes, Kruchenykh presented dialogue and song in a similar paradigmatic construction: an invented syntax and grammar, the basic units of which were disjointed sentences and words and dissonant vowels and consonants dispersed in time.

Divesting the word of its semantic expression, creating a new language of pure sound, and deforming grammatical order, Kruchenykh stripped language of one dimension: meaning. The word became a two-dimensional construct of sound and texture. When meaning did surface, it evolved from comprehensible associations of sound and vocal texture just as the subject in Cubist painting evolved from associations of shapes and visual texture.

Russia hosted the first Cubist theatrical spectacle. A collaboration of young Russian artists, writers, and musicians, the Union of Youth produced *Victory Over the Sun* in the revolutionary spirit of Cubism: free of conventional and traditional perceptions; inventing personal, esoteric languages; and separating substance from expression. Crude and rudimentary, the production precipitated a theatrical style that would eventually be perfected by another Russian producer, Vsevolod Meyerhold.

In the interval between *Victory Over the Sun* and Meyerhold's Cubistic productions of the 1920s, there occurred another theatrical collaboration which brought Cubism on stage: Diaghilev's production of the ballet *Parade,* in Paris, in 1917, with music by Erik Satie, libretto by Jean Cocteau, and designs by Pablo Picasso.

3

Parade (1917) and Before

Before *Parade*

The interval between *Victory Over the Sun,* staged at St. Petersburg in 1913, and *Parade,* staged in Paris, 1917, did not pass without some Cubist stage decoration or costume design. As early as 1914, Natalia Goncharova and, later, Mikhail Larionov designed Cubistic set pieces and costumes for the Russian impressario, Serge Diaghilev. The scenery and costumes for Diaghilev's early productions were colorful, lush creations conceived so that the decorations fused with the costumes; in this fusion, the costumes became integral, mobile parts of the decor. These designs created a plastic unity, a merger of color and form, which would eventually be perfected by Delaunay, Picasso, and Léger in their work for the theatre.

Goncharova and Larionov assimilated the stylistic devices of modern European art movements in their stage designs. For example, Goncharova's decor and costumes for Rimsky-Korsakov's *Le Coq d'Or* (1914), and Larionov's designs for Prokofieff's *Le Chout* (1916–21) synthesized Cubist techniques and Russian primitivism.

Goncharova combined the flattened, simplistic patterns and strong organic colors of Russian peasant art with a Cubist architectonic construction. The background and set pieces for Act I of *Le Coq d'Or* were essentially tall, straight-lined constructions with conical tops representing buildings in a Russian village. The rectangular edifices that made up the background were placed side by side and flattened out in a horizontal line across the back of the stage. Buildings placed in the foreground at either side of the stage had the same rectangular, hard-edged construction and appeared to be extensions of the walls in the background. Overhead, primitively drawn clouds and a red sun fitted into the flattened perspective, as did the several trees and plants scattered over the stage or painted on the backdrop. These forms were decorated with strong, earthy reds, yellows, greens, and blues, as well as floral and animal icons inspired by Russian folk design.

Goncharova designed the costumes on a similar principle: flat patterns from Russian folk art embellished with richly colored floral designs. The broad, planar aprons, skirts, pantaloons, and tunics resembled the rectangular, flat constructions of the background and set pieces; dressed in these costumes, the actors blended into the cubified and colorful background and appeared as mobile parts of the scenery. Goncharova produced a formalistic fusion of background and foreground and an increase in the two-dimensional impression of the stage picture. That these designs were modeled after Cubism became evident when Goncharova remarked: "Cubism is a beautiful, if not entirely new, thing. The Scythian statues, the painted wooden dolls...are made in a Cubist manner."[1]

Cubism had a greater influence on Larionov's designs for *Le Chout*. The Cubist element was so thoroughly developed in these designs that had *Le Chout* been produced in 1916, when Larionov completed the drawings, it would have been a stylistic link between *Victory Over the Sun* and *Parade*.

Larionov began the work on *Le Chout* in 1915, although the ballet, with music by Prokofieff, was actually performed in Paris six years later. Larionov combined several Cubist devices, including primitivism—probably more of an indication of his interest in Russian Neo-Primitivism than Cubism—and simultaneity in the design for "The Merchant's Garden" scene. The sky was depicted in three moods simultaneously: storm clouds, yellow rays of sunlight, and a rainbow. The rendering of the sky closely resembled Cubist stereometric drawings on flattened planes, the picture surface being carved into multifaceted, heavily contoured geometric shapes.

Larionov used a similar pictorial device in the costumes. The costume for a ballerina was constructed in such a way that, from a frontal view, the spectator saw the back and front panels and ornaments of the gown all at once, as well as the undergarments beneath the full skirt. The costume was conceived as one architectural construction of masses and volumes and included a typographical element, the number "2," on one of the panels of the apron.

Other costumes showed similar Cubistic features, particularly those for certain male and female dancers. Both costumes faceted the dancers' bodies into a number of rectangular and cylindrical sections; these were then decorated with geometric shapes such as triangles and spheres in the costume for the male and more primitivist patterns for the female. Photographs of these two dancers against the Cubistically rendered backdrop showed that Larionov achieved the same formalistic fusion of scenic elements that Goncharova achieved in *Le Coq d'Or*. The geometric and primitivist designs of the costumes echoed and blended with the designs of the scenery, giving the stage picture an overall pictorial unity comparable to that in Cubist painting.

Parade (1917)

Despite the Cubistic treatment Malevich and his colleagues gave *Victory Over the Sun*, despite the Cubistic scenery and costumes Goncharova and Larionov rendered for Diaghilev's productions, Pablo Picasso has been generally credited with first bringing Cubism to the theatre. The production was a "surreal" ballet, *Parade,* for which Picasso designed the front curtain, scenery, and costumes.

Russian designer Leon Bakst labeled *Parade* "a Cubist ballet," and Guillaume Apollinaire indicated that *Parade* gave "Cubism concrete form" because it was the first time that painting and movement were successfully and fully united on stage.[2] According to Apollinaire, the productions before *Parade* united decoration and choreography by "factitious bonds," but the Cubist ballet, being a sign of a "New Spirit," joined painting and movement, sculpture and mime, in an "analytic synthesis."[3] Apollinaire used the term "surrealism" to describe the innovative interaction between scenery, choreography, music, and text[4] and proclaimed that Cubism, already a great influence on the pictorial arts since 1907, entered the theatre in 1917 as a prophecy of "a more comprehensive art to come."[5]

Produced by Serge Diaghilev for Les Ballet Russes, *Parade* was conceived by the poet Jean Cocteau in collaboration with the composer Erik Satie; once Diaghilev decided to finance the project, he commissioned Leonide Massine as choreographer, then contracted Pablo Picasso in 1916 to design sets and costumes. Picasso won the commission probably at the insistence of Cocteau and Massine, who believed that the "literalism" of Cubism would counterbalance the ethereal treatment favored by Diaghilev.[6] Picasso joined Cocteau and some young Futurist painters in Rome in 1917 to prepare the designs.

The idea for Cocteau's libretto came from a French definition of the word *parade:* "A comic act put on at the entrance of a traveling theater to attract a crowd."[7] A parody of a traveling circus, the scene for the ballet was the entrance to a tent erected on a Parisian boulevard; an Acrobat, an American Girl, and a Chinese Conjuror performed bits of their routines outside the tent in order to entice pedestrians into purchasing tickets for the show.

Although Picasso had been commissioned only to design the decor and costumes, he managed to bring about a major alteration in Cocteau's script. Cocteau originally planned to give the ballet a mystical or ethereal treatment; "after each musichall turn an anonymous voice, issuing from a kind of megaphone...sang a type-phrase summing up the different aspects of the characters, and opening a breach into the world of dreams."[8] Picasso, however, wanted the ballet to re-create the earthy ribaldry, satire, and flavor of a typical Parisian boulevard spectacle. He suggested that large, mobile scenic structures introduce the various acts and replace certain sound effects, gibberish and nonsensical dialogue called for in Cocteau's original script. Picasso handed Cocteau several sketches for the cardboard costumes, or body masks, to be worn by the dancers who played circus barkers. Cocteau approved Picasso's suggestion, then altered the text to include circus managers in the scenario.

Cocteau's final script called for a French barker who introduced a Chinese Conjuror; the Conjuror performed a comic skit in which he pulled an egg from his braids and ate it. Then the American Manager introduced a little American Girl who rode a bicycle, impersonated Charlie Chaplin, danced a jazz routine, bought a Kodak camera, and quivered like a movie. The last act was introduced by a horse who announced two acrobats. All three ploys failed to draw an audience, and the ballet concluded with the collapse of the three barkers.

Picasso's Designs

Picasso painted a drop curtain to conceal the stage while the orchestra played Satie's overture. Painted on the curtain was a phantasmagorical circus scene in which six theatrical persons, one winged fairy, a winged mare and her colt, a monkey on a ladder, and a sleeping dog lounged amidst stone ruins and plush velvet curtains. The painting was done in a decorative, naive naturalistic fashion and acted as a startling contrast to the stark Cubist set behind the proscenium.

A booth stage had been placed center stage at the rear; it was flanked on both sides and from behind by skyscrapers with windows and by trees on the right. The peak of the booth jutted off to the left into the mass of buildings; two balustrades spread diagonally outward from either end of the proscenium. These set pieces were designed according to a typical Cubist scheme: flattened rectangles and triangles stacked into a two-dimensional architectonic assemblage. The booth in the foreground merged with the angular masses of the background and the deflated volumes of the spherical foliage to the right. The entire set was "cubistically conceived as a sum of factual elements" and "composed in flat synthetic cubist planes"[9] so that objects were immediately recognized.

Picasso's design for the scenery closely resembled his paintings of 1915 and 1916. In an effort to curtail abstraction, Picasso reintroduced literal aspects of the subject; he retained both the formal devices of Synthetic Cubism and some semblance of the realistic appearances of objects. The booth, skyscraper, and trees contained characteristics of Synthetic Cubism but were clearly described.

The dancers entered the stage in turns from the booth and performed their routines on the stage floor. The costumes were basically of two types: typical circus attire and the huge, mobile architectonic body masks. The circus performers (i.e., Chinese Conjuror, American Girl, and Acrobats) dressed in the circus garb and were referred to as "real" or "chromo" group; the "Managers" or barkers wor the huge body masks.

The costume for the Chinese Conjuror consisted of a tunic—a red cloth decorated with yellow stripes and white spirals—which partially covered black trousers with bold, curvilinear stripes, and a red, yellow, and black pointed hat. The "Little American Girl" dressed in a sailor jacket and white pleated skirt and clipped a large white bow in her hair. The Acrobats wore white tights decorated with blue lines and swirls. Cocteau's first scenario included only one Acrobat, but Massine added a second, a female, at the last moment; Picasso created her costume "on the spot" by painting directly on the white fleshings she wore over her body.

The "chromo" performers were introduced by the bizarre, nonhuman Managers; it seemed that these characters were walking Cubist canvases because their appearance derived directly from the paintings and sketches Picasso produced between 1914 and 1916. Described as "Cubist dance masks," the Managers' costumes closed the visual separation between set and actor, "the gap between a nonillusionist set designed as picture-writing and the natural presence of bodies."[10] The Managers were, according to Cocteau, set-pieces given human attributes; it was their nature to stomp around the stage like vulgar automatons, clumsy and out of place with the live dancers.

Matching on stage to the beat of wooden clappers were two ten-foot Cubist constructions of wood and papier-mâché. The French Manager, its placard torso painted blue, white, green, and red, consisted of two panels. The front panel contained a Cubist drawing of a moustached man in formal attire; rendered on the back panel was a silhouette of buildings and trees lining a boulevard. The French Manager carried a walking stick in the right hand and a long, white pipe affixed to an artifical left limb. The American Manager was an equally tall Cubist construction and depicted a cityscape of towering building, clouds, top-hat, Western boots, pleated shirt, flags, and a sign that read "Parade." A megaphone was attached to a long cylindrical arm, and the trousers were made of flat cardboard sheets hinged at the knees.

The Managers were a mix of painting, sculpture, and theatrical costume. Composed of posters, stovepipes, cardboard, and found objects and carried by dancers whose movements were largely determined by the size, weight, and shape of the monolithic masks, the Managers' costumes were Cubist collages put in motion. Containing stereotypical features of American and French cultures, the huge masks functioned as condensed architectonic emblems, as condensed signs of American and French attitudes.

Picasso's interest in building these two edifices was to exaggerate the contrast between the "real" or "chromo" performers, who appeared as miniscule paste-ons against the Cubistic set, and the mammoth, mobile Cubist body masks. The real performers were reduced by the contrast to the scale of puppets. This contrast continued a theatrical application of a vision Picasso nurtured in his Cubist work prior to 1916: Real and invented elements, when simultaneously juxtaposed on one surface, produced an exaggerated sense of reality. Placing the nonhuman, mechanical stature of the Managers against the miniature stature of the doll-like "chromos," Picasso made the dancers unreal and the Managers real in the theatrical context. Schwartz refers to this contrast as "a false scenic reality."[11] and Kozloff describes the juxtaposition as a "charade" that had "as much reality and consequence as the way events actually happen."[12]

Picasso treated Naturalistic and Cubistic approaches as complementary visions, simultaneously accentuating the similarities and differences between them to create a new reality. Picasso worked toward what Rischbieter calls a "painter's theatre" in which the scenery became an autonomous and predominant element.[13] Joseph Carey called it a "true theatre" because its effectiveness issued from the scenery and costumes; all other elements were subservient to the "mobile matter."[14] Creating the Managers, Picasso produced a mise-en-scène that diminished the importance and scale of the actor/dancer and became an independent functioning entity. The American and French Managers not only supplied the stage picture with strong referential Cubist motifs but, as mobile parts of the mise-en-scène, created a new reality, "a false scenic reality," in which objects overwhelmed performers; it was the American and French Managers that made *Parade* "true theatre."

Originally, Cocteau included a third Manager, a black mannikin on a horse. The horse consisted of a yellow canopy draped over two actors, one acting as the head, neck, and front legs and the other as the torso and rear legs. Picasso sculpted a large Negroid doll dressed in formal attire to ride the horse. The back of the horse weakened during rehearsals and the dummy eventually broke off, never to be remounted. The horse, unlike the American and French Managers, looked less like an assemblage of Cubist motifs than a typical circus prop used in clown routines.

Cubistic Choreography

Traveling from Paris to Rome, where the collaborators prepared the production, Picasso was known to have taken an active interest in the choreography for the ballet, particularly in group formations and stereotypical balletic movement. Picasso's interest was revealed in the number of drawings he made of the stylized balletic gestures and poses. The extent of Picasso's contribution to Massine's choreography is not known, but Werner Spies suggests that it was practically impossible to separate Picasso's influence on the style and manner of dancing from this stage designs.[15] This was particularly the case with the Manager costumes, for their construction certainly affected the mobility of those dancers who carred them around the stage.

Whatever has been written about potential motion in Synthetic Cubist painting can be applied to the actual movement of the Managers. This is the conclusion Max Kozloff comes to when he writes: the Managers "contrived to illustrate that inhibited and uncanny motion, that special aspect of made objects come alive, incipient in the Cubist vision of the human figure."[16]

Movement in Cubism was implied by the construction of the figure. Picasso's *Harlequin* (1915), for example, was a stiff, vertical construction composed essentially of a sequence of flat, rectangular planes. Kozloff describes the movement one might expect from this figure:

> ...this harlequin can be as mobile as a rocking horse. We have already seen such movement in Cubism: jerky, tilted, out of kilter, metronomic, wound-up in some peculiar way, as if the image were a clockwork mechanism.[17]

And later, Kozloff refers to the "ironlike clangor" of the Cubistic figure "incapable of motion except that of a mannikin...."[18]

Given the vertical, stiff, and monolithic construction of the Managers, it could have been assumed that their movements actualized what was only a potential or incipient motion in Picasso's *Harlequin*. Cocteau reported that the Managers were "a sort of human scenery, animated portraits by Picasso, and their very structure necessitates a certain choreographic formula."[19]

Descriptions of the Managers' movements invariably refer to a metronomic or clockwork motion. Douglas Cooper writes that the Managers were "reduced to automatons"[20]; Margaret Crosland describes the Managers as "walking pieces of machinery or robots,"[21] and both Cooper and Grigoriev refer to figures who "had to do a lot of stamping, which was intended to suggest conversations between them."[22] Leon Bakst, writing in

1917, described the dance as "an imaginative and very well-thought-out series of jerkily interrupted movements."[23]

Each of these descriptions mentions a hard-edged, mechanical or staccato motion and, in this way, supports Kozloff's description of an incipient "jerky, tilted, out of kilter, metronomic, wound-up" movement in Cubist painting.

Whether Picasso had such movements in mind when he designed the Managers' costumes is uncertain. It is also possible that this effect was not at all intentional since the dancers actually rehearsed without the heavy costumes and were directed to perform more lyrical movements; when the dancers finally put the costumes over their bodies, their movements "lost all their lyric force...."[24] Yet, if Kozloff is correct in saying that movement in Cubist painting was determined by the construction of the figure, it would seem that perhaps Picasso had preconceived "a certain choreographic formula," a Cubistic choreography, when he designed the Managers' costumes.

A Cubistic Score

Erik Satie's music, coupled with the overlay of special sound effects, produced a score which had certain formalistic similarities to Cubist painting and collage. Reacting against the melodious and harmonious styles of Wagner and Tchaikovsky, Satie employed isolated fragments of incomplete melodies to create pulsating patterns of recurring rhythms, to create a syncopated jazz. Cocteau wanted to lay a schema of noise over Satie's composition, hoping to create a sonorous equivalent to Picasso's startling visuals. Picasso, however, managed to persuade Cocteau not to include "suggestive noises and vocal effects," such as the "fugue of footsteps" which was intended for the French and American Managers.[25] Diaghilev also rejected Cocteau's attempt to give the scenery actual voices.

Cocteau then devised a series of mechanical sounds to give the production a modern flair as well as strong auditory references to the atmosphere of Parisian boulevards. Cocteau may have taken this idea from the Futurist noise music, yet it could also have been explained as the equivalent of found objects in Cubism: by employing found objects, the Cubists increased the referential value of their paintings.

Cocteau's idea was twofold. First, each character was to be identified by a certain sound: the Chinese Conjuror by wheels and klaxon; the American Girl by whistles and drum beats; the Acrobats by whip snaps, pistol shots, and percussion; and the Managers by wooden clappers and stamping feet. The collage of sound was to include general background noise, such as typewriters, sirens, telegraph signals, dynamos, and the noise of airplanes.

These sounds Cocteau called "ear deceivers," which he intended to use "with the same object as the 'eye deceivers'—newspapers, comics, imitation woodwork which the painters use."[26] Most of Cocteau's "ear deceivers" were eventually eliminated because they either proved to be technically impracticable or upset Satie, who then converted the noises into instruments. Those that remained, the typewriters for example, were ineffective simply because they could scarcely be heard over the orchestra.

What was significant about Cocteau's plan was that it represented the extension of the Cubist sensibility into sound. The sound collage would have incorporated found noise to increase the literal evocation of the scene; referring to particular objects in the environment, the noises would have functioned as compact signs and recognizable signs of the mechanical age in general and of the urbanscape in particular. Noise could have been regarded as the equivalent of the individual planes and volumes used by the Cubist painters to describe both the particular and general aspects of the subject. Cocteau's sound collage, had it been technically feasible, would have given *Parade* a sonorous equivalent to Cubist pictorial structure.

4

Vsevolod Meyerhold and
the Cubist Theatre

Meyerhold and Cubism

The stylistic similarities between Constructivist art and the scenography for
several productions staged by Vsevolod Meyerhold during the twenties led
historians such as Mordecai Gorelik, Nikolai Gorchakov, and Edward
Braun to classify these years as Meyerhold's Constructivist period. Meyerhold's scaffolds and set pieces for productions such as *The Magnificent
Cuckold* and *The Death of Tarelkin* resembled Constructivist sculpture
with their skeletal wood frames, levels, platforms, and ramps joined and
intersecting in freestanding constructions.

The scenography for many of Meyerhold's so-called "Constructivist"
stagings and non-Constructivist stagings also contained Cubist pictorial
devices. An examination of productions on either side of the Constructivist
period demonstrates that Cubism made its way into Meyerhold's theatrical
aesthetics as early as 1918, in Malevich's set design for *Mystery Bouffe,*
and as late as 1924, in *Give Us Europe.* Paradoxically, Meyerhold's most
comprehensive Cubist statement was made in one of his most celebrated
Constructivist stagings: his production of Crommelynck's *The Magnificent
Cuckold* in 1922 and 1928.

To point out the Cubist elements in Meyerhold's Constructivist productions is not to deny that these productions had Constructivist elements
but simply to isolate and identify those elements of his productions that
had their artistic counterparts or equivalents in Cubist painting. Where it is
necessary to distinguish between Constructivist and Cubist elements, it will
be explained in what ways the production was at variance with a Constructivist aesthetics and conformed to a Cubist aesthetics.

Meyerhold had a perpetual and practicable interest in the fine arts
throughout his career and frequently used reproductions of paintings to
arrange movements, gestures, and group formations.*[1] It was possible that

Meyerhold came into contact with reproductions of Cubist paintings through a number of sources: Serge Diaghilev published reviews and reproductions of contemporary art in his journal, *The World of Art;* Fernand Léger frequently exhibited his work in Moscow galleries; and *Du Cubisme* by Gleizes and Metzinger was translated and published in Russia shortly after its publication in France.

By 1920, at the latest, Meyerhold had been impressed by Cubism and considered a future collaboration with Cubist artists. He remarked in 1920, "We are right to invite Cubists to work with us, because we need settings which resemble those we shall be performing against tomorrow."[2] Cubist elements regularly appeared in Meyerhold's productions over the next four years, in settings for *The Dawns* (1920), *Mystery Bouffe* (1921), *The Magnificent Cuckold* (1922), *The Death of Tarelkin* (1922), *Forest* (1924), and *Give Us Europe* (1924). Meyerhold organized the stage picture for these productions in much the same way Picasso and Braque organized the pictorial surface in their Cubist paintings.

Meyerhold was, like Picasso and Braque, primarily concerned with an *aesthetics or technique of production* rather than with disseminating an ideology or social doctrine. Mordecai Gorelik wrote that Meyerhold's major contribution to the Russian stage was to reinstate an aesthetics of the "theatre theatrical."[3] Just as Cubist painters made the *painting as an independent reality* important, the painting painterly, Meyerhold made the *production as an independent reality* important, the "theatre theatrical." While the Cubists concerned themselves first with a means of painting, not illusionism or psychologism, Meyerhold concerned himself with the means of staging and not realism or naturalism. The staging was, in effect, the content; and, just as the Cubists sacrificed realistic portrayals of the subject to abstract configuration, Meyerhold sacrificed the playscript to a mode of production, to theatricality.

Picasso and Braque saw perspectivism as a means of diminishing reality; similarly, Meyerhold looked on naturalism as a means of reducing reality to a narrow, confined viewpoint. He used the term "schematization" to refer to "a certain impoverishment of reality, as though it somehow entailed the reduction of its totality."[4] Naturalism schematized reality in the way that illusionism diminished nature, and while the Cubist painters developed a style of painting that synthesized perspective as a reaction to illusionism, Meyerhold developed a "synthetical"[5] production aesthetics as an alternative to naturalism.

Meyerhold sought a visual synthesis through all aspects of production. In *The Dawns,* for example, he employed Cubist shapes in the set and costumes to create a formalistic dialogue between the scenographic elements and the actors; the mise-en-scène for *The Magnificent Cuckold* functioned as one homogenous form, one expressive substance, in which the design of the set and costumes resembled the two-dimensional landscape of geometric forms found in Cubism. Meyerhold's intention paralleled that of the Cubists: to eliminate the distinction between substance and form, background and foreground, and scene and figure.

While the Cubist painters ignored principles of perspectivism, Meyerhold ignored naturalistic devices. He was initially influenced in this objective by Georg Fuchs, whose book, *The Theatre of the Future,* was published in Berlin in 1904 or 1905. Meyerhold read Fuchs' book in 1906 and used it as a source book for his theoretical pursuits toward a new staging aesthetics. Fuchs' book contained an adamant rejection of naturalism, particularly scenic naturalism, and affected Meyerhold in the way that Cézanne's paintings affected Picasso and Braque: Fuchs, like Cézanne, believed that background and foreground should be joined in a formalistic unity.

Inspired by Goethe's idea to combine in the scenic work the skills of the architect and the painter, Fuchs envisioned a new scenic artist, a "space artist," whose task was "to think concretely. . .in three dimensions so as to be able to subject the decorative and pictorial elements to the dramatic substance of the theatre."[6] Fuchs' theories led him to experiment with the relief-stage, which he felt was "the spatial form. . .in accordance with drama itself, its innate law and its means of expression."[7]

Although the relief-stage separated the actor from the background, preventing the formalistic integration of foreground with background, its shallow stage with the actor placed close in front prefigured the formalistically integrated stage picture Meyerhold created in productions such as *The Magnificent Cuckold.* Eliminating the proscenium, Fuchs left only two planes on stage: the playing area and, pushed tight against it, the backdrop. In his production of *Hamlet* at the Kunstlertheater in Munich, in 1901, Fuchs pressed his actors against the scenic backdrop, creating an impression of a flattened and shallow pictorial surface. A palace guard, for example, appeared to be situated on the same plane as the turrets on the palace wall behind him; he seemed to have height and width only.

Spurred by Georg Fuchs' rejection of naturalism as well as his own successful experiments in Symbolism, Meyerhold continued to explore innovative, nonrepresentational staging methods. Meyerhold accelerated his radical experiments while acting as director of the branch Studio of the Moscow Art Theatre, and it eventually became apparent that his "theatre theatrical" was irreconcilably opposed to Stanislavsky's representational methods. Meyerhold's grievance with naturalism echoed the Cubists' complaint against illusionism: naturalism confused form and content, and, in perfecting representational forms, "transformed art into photography."[8]

Fuchs' theories and work not only corroborated Meyerhold's rejection of naturalism but also pointed out the disparity between the three-dimensional human figure and the two-dimensional painted scenic backdrop. Using Fuchs' ideas as a model for a production of *Ghosts* in 1906, Meyerhold "removed the front curtain, built a deep forestage and employed a single constructed (not painted) setting."[9] The production of *Tristan and Isolde* (1909) continued this interest in closing the visual distance between actor and background; Meyerhold placed the actors in plastic groupings against relief settings so that the patterns and figures of the groups repeated the bold architectonic patterns and shapes in the set behind them.

Meyerhold's early experiments with Fuchs' theories obviously could not be classified as Cubistic endeavors; to classify them as Cubist would be to claim that Fuchs and Meyerhold predated Picasso and Braque in creating Cubism. There were stark differences between Meyerhold's early work and that of the twenties, principally in the use of representational scenery and costumes; although the plastic groupings in *Tristan and Isolde* displayed a formal affinity with the relief setting, the actors' movements were designed after Symbolist or Oriental models of rhythmical movement. In short, Meyerhold did not, in the early productions, produce a total, geometricized synthesis of the entire mise-en-scène.

These early productions are, however, relevant to this study because they reveal the early phases in Meyerhold's evolution toward Cubist staging. They reveal a conceptual or doctrinal parallel between Meyerhold's rejection of naturalism and his experiments with Fuchs' theories and the Cubists' rejection of representationalism and their early experiments with Cézannian "passage." It was out of his experiments with Fuchs' conception of relief-staging that Meyerhold comprehended the inherent contradiction between the three-dimensional human figure and the two-dimensional background.

Meyerhold's work on several productions during the 1920s paralleled the Cubists' endeavor to overcome the conflict between structure and representation. Theatricality was, for Meyerhold, the antithesis of nature and he worked to free artistic invention of the contradiction between representation and structure; he worked in the theatre toward a conceived reality. The manner in which he resolved this contradiction resulted in a stylistic affinity with Cubism.

Mystery Bouffe (1918, 1921)

Analytic Cubism was the label given to Cubist paintings produced between 1906 and 1912. In this period, Picasso and Braque dissected and fragmented their subjects into objective forms and reorganized the underlying geometric construction of objects and the environs into an architectonic assemblage. Meyerhold achieved a theatrical equivalent to Analytic Cubism in the architectonic set for his production of *Mystery Bouffe* by Vladimir Mayakovsky.

Meyerhold assigned Kasimir Malevich to design the set and costumes for the original production at the Theatre of Musical Drama in Petrograd in 1918. Malevich conceived the set as "a cubistic picture" consisting of a huge blue hemisphere to represent earth and several cubes to depict an ark; these large geometric solids were placed in front of geometrical backcloths. The costumes for the proletariat in this production consisted of uniform grey overalls. These designs did not please Mayakovsky for he drew another set of more colorful and individualized costumes.

When the production was revived in 1921, at the First Theatre of the R.S.F.S.F. in Moscow, V. Kisselyov, A. Lavinsky and V. Khrakovsky were commissioned to design the costumes and set. Although Lavinsky and Khrakovsky's plan for the set was more representational than Malevich's plan, it still showed strong Cubistic elements.

The enormous blue hemisphere filled most of the downstage area; it revolved on a broad ramp and had a wedge cut out of its side to depict an exit from Hell. Platforms, ramps, poles, ropes, and stairways were constructed in front of the backdrop of vertical rectangles which represented the deck of a steamship; these structures were also used to signify a number of other locales during the production.

Meyerhold removed the front curtain from the proscenium and thrust the hemisphere and the downstage platform onto the apron, close to the front row of seats in the auditorium. All the stage pieces were built tight against one another in a vertical assemblage that seemed to rise up steeply on the forestage. Although Meyerhold accentuated the massive qualities of these set pieces by thrusting them forward, he also created a foreshortened and tilted stage picture by compressing the several structures in the vertical assemblage.

The set pieces were actually several independent geometric forms and rectilinear planes joined to make an architectonic construction. As in Analytic Cubist paintings, the edges of the various shapes and levels were boldly marked and rigid. In the assemblage, the stacked geometric solids were pushed tightly against one another, but each structure retained its independent visual identity through the well-defined contours. These set pieces depicted various locales but appeared as quasi-representational geometric forms; the set, then, did not merely create "place" but also served as an independent visual image consisting of geometric volumes and planes joined in and filling the stage space. As in Analytic Cubism, the subject was depicted in essential, underlying geometric shapes: the underlying *shapes embraced the content; the content, in turn, acted as a paradigm for the geometric identity of the shapes.*

Stacked one on top of the other in a vertical, tight construction, the platforms, ramps, and cubes seemed to scale one another and crowd the picture surface. The *Mystery Bouffe* set resembled the architectonic vertical assemblage in Braque's *Houses at L'Estaque.* Just as the pile of geometric shapes in Braque's painting not only described the subject but also filled the canvas, the assemblage of rectilinear platforms and planes filled the entire stage; as in Cubist paintings, the stage architecture became a pictorial, plastic environment.

Kisselyov created the costumes for this production and dressed the proletariat in blue overalls. The capitalists wore more colorful Cubistic outfits, which resembled the drawings Mayakovsky made when he became displeased with Malevich's designs. James Symons describes the "two-*dimension, posterlike effect"*[10] the costumes gave to the actors, and Braun writes that the costumes "had something of the pith and vigor" of "the most telling political posters of the early Soviet period...."[11]

The set and costumes for Meyerhold's next production, *The Dawns,* were given a similar Cubistic treatment. The Cubist elements were, however, developed to a greater extent, particularly in the set and stage properties, so that a slight, rudimentary surface/depth dialogue took place between the foreground and background.

The Dawns (1920)

An epic verse drama written by Emile Verhaeren in 1898, *The Dawns* dramatized the transformation of a fictitious capitalist war into an international proletarian revolution in the mythical town of Oppidomane. Meyerhold adapted Verhaeren's script and used the production to commemorate the Third Anniversary of the October Revolution and to inaugurate the First Theatre of the R.S.F.S.R.

In an article on staging *The Dawns,* Meyerhold and his assistant, Valery Bebutov, mentioned that the production made them "kindred spirits" with Picasso and Tatlin since their concern in building the set was related to the concerns of the two artists in their work: "the art of manufacturing."[12] They cared little about creating attractive pictorial effects; rather they wanted to "hack stage sets out of the materials of raw nature" and replace "pretty patterns and colours" with "the juxtaposition of the surfaces and shapes of *tangible materials!"*[13]

Given the condition of the old dilapidated building, it would seem that the producers had little choice but to hack at the raw materials. The theatre was an ancient ransacked edifice, its auditorium unheated, its plaster peeling from the walls, and its chairs falling apart. Meyerhold, however, believed it to be a perfect setting for the production, and when critics suggested that the production should be moved to a better equipped theatre, he sharply replied:

> We would be glad to offer Verhaeren's *The Dawns* to the [Moscow] Art Theatre and let them review their own repertoire. If they decide it is necessary for them to change their repertoire we will give them this play, choose another work and strive to introduce even more cubism, suprematism, and tear out even more footlights.[14]

Meyerhold invited a former student in his theatre classes in Petrograd to design the scenery and costumes. Vladimir Dmitriev produced a Cubist, contra-relief set, placing multi-colored geometric and voluminous forms against a painted backdrop of geometric designs.

One of these Cubistic settings consisted of vertically piled, stark geometric structures dispersed across the stage. These structures were occasionally shaded with dark contrasts producing massive indentations of volume on the frontal planes of the cubic boxes. The largest structure was a lopsided cube at stage right. Protruding from the top of this cube was a short, broad cylinder and to the rear two triangular extensions and an enormous, metallic ring. Two cones, one small, one large, appeared behind the large cube, the smaller cone situated in front of a large triangular form. To the left of the triangular form was a low pyramid that was flanked on the left by a cube with triangular and spherical markings on its front side. Behind this conglomeration of red, gold, and metallic cubes, discs, cylinders, and pyramids was a pattern of similar geometric shapes, as well as cross-hatched ropes and triangles cut from sheets of tin.

Dmitriev's intention was not to represent the city of Oppidomane but to give merely an impression of it. Keeping with Meyerhold's interest in tangible materials of raw nature, the designer constructed the scenery from iron, metal, wood, and rope, occasionally placing recognizable objects, such as gates and crosses, in front of the nonobjective geometric forms. Using raw materials and recognizable objects, Dmitriev was able to describe the city despite the abstract nature of the other pieces of scenery.

The costumes and stage props were also designed and constructed in geometric schematization, and, in this way, they reflected the patterns and lines in the set pieces and backdrop. The suits of armor worn by soldiers were made of painted canvas and decorated as geometric patchworks, having voluminous cylinders for sleeves and legs; broad planes joined in a line at the waist to cover the torso. The conical head of the spears and the curved shields carried by the soldiers looked as though they had been sliced from the geometric patterns in the background.

The civilians wore flat-topped caps and large pieces of fabric which, stitched and painted to emphasize the seams and contours, accentuated the planar expanse of the shoulders, the cylindrical construction of the legs and arms, and the binary, rectangular construction of the back. The civilian men wore jodphurs which were flared and flattened. The civilian women concealed their bodies under voluminous, full skirts, giving the lower anatomy a cylindrical appearance and, by contrast, the upper anatomy a more planar quality.

Meyerhold moved the playing area forward as he did in *Mystery Bouffe*. Placing the actor closer to the auditorium and moving the setting forward, Meyerhold hoped the actor would blend into the stage picture, merge with the scenery, so that the formalistic similarities in set and costume might produce a close correspondence to the pictorial effects in Cubism.

This also seemed to be his objective in designing the front curtain, which Meyerhold used, for the last time, to separate the acts. Dmitriev's curtain was, in a sense, a foreword to the Cubistic set behind it. On a blank background, Dmitriev designed an imperfect red circle that was perforated on the right by a large, triangular yellow wedge and inscribed with the letters RSFSR. Although this design also resembled Malevich's Suprematist paintings, it served as a clue to the Cubistic decor and Cubistic pictorial scheme behind the curtain.

Dmitriev's design was intended, as were Analytic Cubist paintings, to present a suggestion, an abstraction of the subject in its underlying geometric pattern. To reduce the distortion brought about by abstraction, the Cubists introduced either real objects, realistic images, or typographical elements into the scheme of geometric shapes. In a similar way, Meyerhold placed realistic icons over the geometric abstraction to describe the scene. Iron gates indicated an entrance to the city or a building; cemetery crosses denoted a specific location; suits of armor distinguished civilians from soldiers and perhaps a battlefield from a street.

With the production of *The Dawns,* Meyerhold and Dmitriev created a stage picture that had a stylistic affinity to Analytic Cubist paintings. Building the set and costumes from a familial class of geometric forms, thrusting the set forward toward the lip of the stage, placing geometricized figures in front of the geometricized scenery and background, Meyerhold produced a semblance of the flattened picture surface of Cubist paintings. The fusion of forms in the background with forms in the foreground lessened the three-dimensional impression of the stage space and produced a homogenous landscape in which all parts had equal strength. There was, in the repetition and fusion of familial forms in the costumes and scenery, a hint of the surface/depth dialogue in Cubism. This effect was to be perfected in his staging *The Magnificent Cuckold* in 1922.

Despite his attempts to fuse costume and setting, Meyerhold felt that he and Dmitriev failed to integrate completely the abstract design of the background with the stage action. This failure might have been explained by the fact that Meyerhold employed an awkward and inappropriate mixture of movement and gesture. Meyerhold directed his actors to use movements seen in ballet and military drills but made no attempt to integrate these gestures with the geometricized lines and shapes of the Cubistic set. That Meyerhold acknowledged this failure revealed his concern for integrating every aspect of the production into a single stylistic and formal synthesis, into a flattened stage landscape.

The Magnificent Cuckold (1922)

Fernand Crommelynck's play, *The Magnificent Cuckold,* was first staged by Meyerhold in April 1922 and later in January 1928. Crommelynck thought the play could be presented as either a farce or tragedy; Meyerhold favored a farcical treatment, using the playscript as a pretext for an abstract acrobatic staging.

Meyerhold wanted the production to "lay the basis for a new form of theatrical presentation with no need for illusionistic settings or complicated props...."[15] The set design was probably a collaborative effort between himself and his designer Lyubov Popova. Meyerhold probably described what the set should look like and left scale and dimension to Popova.

Meyerhold mounted the production at a time when cloth, paint, metal, and lighting equipment were in short supply. The only material in abundant supply was wood. Meyerhold decided to construct a bare, utilitarian scaffold made of wood rather than repair and paint the flats he found in the old Zon Theatre. He stripped the stage of all structural accessories, including curtain, soffits and cornices, and the fly galleries. All that remained was the enormous proscenium opening, the huge bare stage, and a brick wall at the rear.

On the bare stage, Meyerhold and Popova erected an abstract, three-dimensional construction of platforms, inclined planes and ramps, stairways, a trapeze, slide, discs, and large blades on the end of a pole. The set piece depicted the mill of Crommelynck's protagonist, Bruno. This construction, with its runways, levels, and platforms, was an example of what Fuerst and Hume refer to as *scenic dynamism*. Scenic dynamism, as defined by the two authors, was "the organization of the practicability of the stage, the organization of the stage in terms of levels, inclines and stairs...."[16] They added that construction of this type encouraged directors to organize actors into groups that were then placed on the various levels over the stage directors, such as Meyerhold, to achieve a formalistic integration of actor and set.

There was actually little difference between the spatial organization of Popova's set and the architectonic portrayals of Cubist painting. A significant aspect of Picasso's *Les Demoiselles D'Avignon* and other examples of Cubism was the treatment of space, the three-dimensional, but flattened, design of architectonic forms on the picture plane. Picasso and Braque devised a plan for spatial organization by perfecting Cézanne's technique of "passage," joining or running together planes normally separated in space with the effect of integrating surface and depth. In Picasso's *Houses On A Hill* and Braque's *Houses At L'Estaque,* the massive frontal planes that defined the houses and thick foliage swept in and out of one another, competing for space. The "passage" device created a close knit composition of disparate objects fused into one surface with an inherent depth.

Popova's set for *The Magnificent Cuckold* was designed on a similar plan, using a tightly interlocked spatial system to create a cohesive structure from a mélange of parts. Frontally the set appeared to be a massive conglomeration of planks, boards, and runways. It was a free-standing assemblage of wooden frames and platforms joined by stairways, chutes, ramps, and catwalks. Two trestle platforms spaced approximately ten to twelve feet apart provided the major compartments for the mill and were connected by a slanting walkway. Another plank slanted downward from inside the top of the stage-left structure onto the stage floor and terminated at the foot of the stage-right trestle. The two free-standing trestle platforms were visually connected in space by these two ramps. Two staircases placed at the free ends of each platform slanted inward, seeming to brace the entire scaffold. The outline of the building was a flattened, integrated structure of planes joined together in space, and, in this way, it resembled the fusion of planar houses in Picasso's and Braque's paintings.

The Cubist painters exploited the salient, geometric features of the subject in order to reduce realistic anatomical characteristics to the architectonic basis of its construction. Depicting the subject in its formal elements only, the Cubists were not inclined toward realistic portrayals but toward an intellectualization of the subject. Meyerhold and Popova employed a similar logic in designing the scaffold. Tied together and arranged inside the scaffold frame, the profusion of scattered, intersecting planks and boards crystalized in an abstract, geometric intellectualization of a mill.

Three wheels, the largest painted black with white lettering, were installed behind the skeletal construction. The letters CR ML NCK were printed on the largest wheel to represent the name of the playwright, Crommelynck. Meyerhold removed the proper name, Crommelynck, from its literal, semantic meaning; dissecting the word, or restructuring it, in terms of consonants. Meyerhold pared the word to an architectonic feature so that the letters became a pictorial element having an independent logic and meaning. Reducing and restructuring the word in architectural terms, he recreated the architectural pattern of Popova's scaffold. All elements of the set were consequently synthesized through the basic architectonic forms of objects. Meyerhold, like Picasso and Braque, used architectural design and the synthesis of underlying architectural features as a pretext for composition.

Distilled to an objective, architectonic pretext, the scaffold for *The Magnificent Cuckold* exhibited the rudimentary plastic effect that characterized most of Picasso's and Braque's paintings. The scaffold contained the subject, a miller's house, and the space around it, the village, in one geometricized, invented plastic environment. The free-standing construction appeared to be sculpted yet two-dimensional in the interplay of plastic geometric shapes in the frame. Conceived as an abstract, plastic structure, the scaffold was not bound to literal denotations or connotations but became an object in its own right, having its own absolute value and interest as a newly invented form. It became, like Cubist icons, *object-as-form.*

Placing the underlying basic forms of represented objects in an internal, architectural scheme, the Cubists made these forms the basis of a new, abstract and independent construction. The parts became the building blocks for a new, cubified object, one that fused the content of the subject with the architectural substance of the painted object. The structure of the subject became intelligible only through the ordering and internal collective functioning of the new forms in the invented object. No single part sufficiently described the subject; it was only after a systematic survey of the interaction, the associative value, of all the parts that the cubified object became an intelligible and analogous subject. Meyerhold's scaffold for *The Magnificent Cuckold* also depended on the collective, associative relationship of the internal parts to establish meaning. It was the collective functioning and/or manipulation of the essential features of the scaffold that fused the content of the subject with its architectural substance in space to describe the new object. The subject became intelligible, as it did in Cubism, through the internal functioning of its essential, architectural forms.

The scaffold was placed on a bare stage backed by a brick wall, stripped of all decorative devices and left with only the diagrammatic outline of its skeletal construction and several functional attachments. Above and behind the two towers, the wheels and discs would revolve at varying speeds as indices of the emotional states of characters. Attached to the trestle at the right were two hinged doors; the revolving lower door served as an instrument or weapon when manipulated by the actors. Catwalks and slides were part of the functional, utilitarian design and were used regularly to indicate space or to carry action. In addition, positive and negative spaces on the scaffold were used as doors and windows. The three-dimensional, architectonic scaffold was something to be "passed through, walked round, climbed on, swung on and slid down."[17] Manipulating the parts of the construction, the actors defined the abstract forms, fusing the content with the substance of the assemblage. Meaning emerged from the collective functioning of the parts.

Cubist painters employed a novel device known as *simultaneity* to distort pictorial space and juxtapose the structural features of an object. Simultaneity was the "simultaneous presence in a cubist painting of separate points of view."[18] In *Les Demoiselles D'Avignon,* for example, the squatting figure displayed two anatomical parts not commonly seen at the same time: the broad square back and the face seen frontally. Simultaneity presented the subject in an abnormal perspective, from two or more angles at once.

The theatrical counterpart to Cubist simultaneity presented the object without confining it to realistic or literal references. Meyerhold's unusual application of stage design and action, a device that will be referred to as *transmutable meaning,* constituted a theatrical extension or elaboration of Cubist simultaneity.

Transmutable meaning was the capacity of an object to present "what it is" and more, depending on how it was used in the setting or manipulated by the actor; it was possible for a stage prop or set piece to have one or more possible sets of meanings or perspectives within the production; a single object could simultaneously present two or more independent perspectives or references. Transmutable meaning was, in this way, to stage naturalism what simultaneity was to one-point perspective.

In naturalism, planes, staircases, slides, and doors had a fixed, specific reference. They had literal meanings which could not be violated. The stage property took for its law "the truth of external appearances...."[19]

By contrast, the stage object in Meyerhold's production, the chute for flour sacks, for example, assumed any number of meanings and references depending on how it was manipulated. In one scene, the chute was just that: a slide by which people or objects left the mill. In another scene, the chute became a bed. Likewise, other areas of the set transcended external appearances and assumed roles that the action or psychology suggested. The blades and wheels simultaneously acted as windsails and mill wheels, respectively, and also spun as an indication, a signal, of Bruno's psychological condition. The revolving lower door was at once an entrance and a weapon. In his article, "Meyerhold's Production of *The Magnificent Cuckold*," Nick Worrall aptly summarizes Meyerhold's technique of transmutable meaning:

> What was formerly a closed, linear world...in the forms of stage Naturalism...has become the world of THE MAGNIFICENT CUCKOLD, an open-ended one in which meanings are created in the process of producing oneself and a condition.[20]

While simultaneity enabled the Cubists to enlarge and open perspective, Meyerhold's transmutable meaning extended stage areas and props beyond conventional limitations on structure. Content, or meaning, was not determined by actual form; the object appeared abstract in its open-endedness, existing logically as a concrete entity but "becoming" by its reference, by its contextual implications.

The Futurist artists also employed a technique they referred to as simultaneity, but their notion differed radically from the Cubist notion. In *Cubism/Futurism,* Max Kozloff explains the difference: Cubist simultaneity consisted in "several visual juxtapositions, corresponding to our motor and tactile responses to objects," while the Futurist notion consisted in the indivisible co-existence of opposites.[21]

The Futurist Marinetti published a play in 1915, entitled *Simultaneity,* in which two different settings, inhabited by two different sets of characters, occupied the stage at the same time; although a prop from one setting, a table for example, occupied a part of the other setting, the actors in one setting did not interact with those in the other. The following year, Marinetti employed simultaneity in his play *The Communicating Vases.* Here he placed on stage three unrelated scenes divided by two partitions and called for the action in all three locations to take place concurrently.

In the Futurist theatre, unrelated elements occupied the same general space, the stage seen diachronically in one view, at the same time. Meyerhold used simultaneity to depict a single object, to exhibit different features or meanings of the utilitarian objects yet preserved their formalistic content as both substance and expression.

Props and stage areas derived meaning from usage, through transmutable meaning, creating "sign systems...full of fluctuating content."[22] Like the object in Cubist paintings, the stage object was no longer imitative of a realistic model but embodied its meaning in neutral forms that eventually "became" an identity through the activity on stage. There was a parallel between Meyerhold's use of open forms with a latent, variable content and the use of "condensed signs" in Cubism.

In both Meyerhold's production and Cubist painting, a "condensed sign" was an object in which formal and connotative qualities were synthesized into one characteristic, conventional new form. The new form not only described the subject but also provided a specific context for the objects and areas around it. Objects became, through their associative value, indices or signs for all the qualities normally associated with the object. Gorchakov has remarked that a single flower in the heroine's hand was sufficient to "turn the bare platform into a terrace that was filled with flowers bathed in the morning sun."[23] The red pom-poms that hung from Bruno's neck were "both the sign of the clown and the characteristic decoration on a suit of baby clothes"[24]; when Bruno threw jealous tantrums, the tassels reduced the mature male to a petulant, infantile buffoon. The tassels supplied a strong, interpretative context for the action. This was essentially the function of the caning in Picasso's *Still-Life With Chair-Caning* (1912). The use of actual chair-caning in the painting not only described the conventional visual reality but also, without resort to illusionism, acted as a specific reference for the other objects in the composition; the lemon, glass, oyster, pipe, and newspaper became, by association, articles in a cafe where the chairs had caning for seats.

The Cubist innovation of condensed signs bridged the void between form and content because the object was no longer bound to its literal meaning and structure. Meyerhold made content a variable of "the active power of choice in reversing a previously immutable order"[25]; the meaning of a place, an object, and the things around it were intrinsically connected "with the creation of meanings in a theatrical landscape."[26]

Although Popova's scaffold resembled Constructivist sculptures, it actually functioned at odds with a purist Constructivist aesthetics. Constructivist sculpture was not designed to resemble anything; it had a purely nonrepresentational and utilitarian function. When Meyerhold added recognizable details—windsails, mill wheels, a chute, doors, and windows—he gave the abstract, geometricized assemblage a concrete identity: the scaffold became a mill. In addition, through the functioning of the various parts, "...Popova's contraption evoked inevitable associations with the windmill in which the play was to be set...and...led to an unavoidable compromise of their [Constructivists'] utilitarian dogma...."[27] The operation and manipulation of the parts created, through the associative faculties of the imagination, a specific reference. The identity of the scaffold was established in the same way that the subject was portrayed in Cubist paintings: in reducing realistic appearances to underlying, geometric forms which became "sign systems...full of fluctuating content."[28]

Writing in *The New Spirit in the Russian Theatre,* Huntley Carter mentions that early Constructivist scaffolds were devices for "showing the actor in the round" and that platforms, levels, ramps, and runways gave "higher interpretative value to the movements and speech of the actors."[29]

Meyerhold, who used the actor primarily as a scenic element, not as a discursive vehicle for the text, exploited the "interpretative value" of his actors by manipulating them into pictorial motifs patterned after the design of the scaffold; the stage landscape became a pictorial space which Meyerhold used as the Cubists did: not as a mirror but as a diagram. *The Magnificent Cuckold* was "a manifestation of a collective performance"[30] in which Meyerhold achieved an integrated, nonindividualistic stage action. His actors were organized into group formations or *perceptual areas,* their poses and movements distributed through space in a way that resembled the distribution of line, volume, and plane in Cubist painting.

When opening the boundaries of closed, analytic forms, Picasso and Braque intruded on the contours of forms "in the interest of overall pictorial structure."[31] Inside the conglomeration of parts, there developed areas of concentration that separated the surface of the painting into sections, each section having a specific character, and created contrasts of density, volume, and plane. The effect was to draw the viewer's eye to "perceptual areas" arranged in a "visual gestalt of the highest possible unity."[32] Ultimately a function of the total pictorial effect, the perceptual areas could, at any point, describe the subject or some aspect of it. Yet, when isolated, these areas went beyond mere description to become self-sufficient forms. No longer a guitar, vase, or human profile, the arrangement was so united that it became a new form, a new plane, growing from the old associations; the visual gestalt had a force of its own, a unique and distinctive force growing from the collectivization of individual parts; the individual parts functioned collectively to assume a new form with a single identity.

However strong and independent, the perceptual area was inextricably subservient and contributory to the overall pictorial effect. In this way, the Cubist painters created a number of visual nuclei, a multi-point perspective, integrated within one pictorially consistent structure.

The arrangement of parts into perceptual areas ultimately bound to the interests of a larger effect characterized Meyerhold's manipulation of individual and group dynamics into a "collective performance." The performers in *The Magnificent Cuckold* were, like the parts in certain Cubist paintings, organized into perceptual areas or groups, each having a nucleus independent of the total stage picture. The linkage was generally a pose or stance revealing a linear, curvilinear or acrobatic relation among the several actors.

In one scene, for example, four actors — two on the stage-left trestle and two on the stairs leading to the trestle floor — formed one perceptual area in that each actor represented one part in a four-part sequence. Meyerhold arranged all four actors frontally, with an equal spread between their feet. The first actor in the sequence stood lowest on the stairs; his right knee bent deeply as if to push upward, his back tilted backwards as if ready to spring forward, he prepared to ascend the stairs. His fists were clenched and held above his head.

The actor in front of him assumed a pose that was a continuation of the first. The second actor in the sequence was one step off the platform, but his right knee was bent and his right foot placed squarely on the floor of the platform. His fists were also clenched but held to the side of the head as though they were lowered from the position at which the first actor held his fists. The second actor's body was slightly tilted backwards as if in the process of moving forward onto the platform.

The third actor completed the forward motion since he crouched on top of the trestle. His right knee was bent, a continuation of the second phase. His body was bent at the waist and followed the right arm, which was held out straight with the right hand pointing across the catwalk to the other trestle. The left arm was held out behind and below the waist as though it had been lowered and pushed outward from the head.

The fourth actor completed the sequence. He crouched low to the floor and was tensed as though the body had absorbed the impact of a lunge forward. The left arm was held out behind him, but it was placed above the waist as if it had been lifted from the position at which the third actor held his left arm. The left fist was clenched like the fists of the first actor. The right arm and hand pointed outward, slanting downward but still across the catwalk to the other platform, in the same direction that the third actor pointed.

Seen as a four-part sequence, as the individual frames of a motion picture, the four actors collectively portrayed one attitude, one gesture, pointing across the catwalk to the other trestle. With her back turned to the line of men, a woman walked erect on the other platform, her right hand continuing the point, stretched upward, toward the end of the scaffold. The outstretched arm linked her pose to that of the men behind her, while her upright stance distinguished her as a separate visual element, making her figure an independent, though related, visual area.

In the same scene, a circle of four actors were arranged on the floor in front of the scaffold. These four performers constituted another independent perceptual area in the staging. Three of the four actors were bathed in light and leaned backwards, supporting their bodies with their back right leg, their left leg pushed out forward and straight. The fourth actor in the group stooped in the shadow, which set him off from the three performers in the light; yet, his rear right leg supported his weight, the left leg forward but bent and his arms held in the same position as the other three: the right arm forward, the left arm behind the right.

To the right of this circle, there was another perceptual area containing two performers: one leaning forward, an echo of the line of actors on the stairs and platform above but connected to the circle of actors by his backward glance and identical arm positions; his right arm stretched out so that his hand seemed to touch the left shoulder of the other actor in this group. The second actor sat on the end of the slide, both arms and legs bent. His head was directed off to the right, connecting him with the performers in the circle, the line on the scaffold, and the woman on the trestle. In this scene alone, there were four independent, though related, gestalts in one field.

The grouping of actors into perceptual areas joined by their stylistic affinities occurred at other moments in the production. During Bruno's nightmare, a crowd of peasant women raised their arms and clubs in unison as a collective gesture of violence:

> They all look threateningly as they lean toward him, each holding aloft a club as if to beat him. The [women] and [Bruno] combine to produce an image of the cuckold surrounded by the phallic images of his own distressed fantasy.[33]

Imperative to the use of perceptual areas was the condition that, while independent gestalts were self-sufficient, they must ultimately interrelate and, as paradigms, contribute to the structural consistency of the entire pictorial structure. Meyerhold choreographed his performers so that their movements and poses were integrated in two ways: by similar or identical gestures and by their iconic affinity to the geometric forms contained in the architecture of the scaffold.

Looking at the four perceptual areas, again, revealed no single gesture or stance in each gestalt that did not relate in some way to the other groups. The four areas were connected visually by arm gestures, body stance, directionality, or sequential progression. The movements and poses of the actors were fully synchronized, each group having individual characteristics of movement or gestures yet ultimately subservient to a group context, to the overall pattern of the scene. "It was as if, separately, each character constituted merely the sign of his identity...and it was only as part of a whole, in action and movement, that their individual presences were flushed out and given meaning and coherence."[34] James Symons has referred to this unity of "external physical dynamics" as "a kind of *gestalt* characterization."[35]

A visual logic emerged from the associations of paradigmatic poses and gestures contained in the various gestalts; this logic emerged not only from the associations of the individual areas but from the association of group gestalts and scaffold. The plastic architecture of the scaffold was repeated in each individual gesture and movement inside the gestalts. The angular, bent legs and arms repeated the pattern of stairs; the extended arms repeated the straight lines of the flat slanted ramps; the body posed in stiff, hard-edged stances repeated the many geometric patterns created in the crossbeams on the frame of the scaffold.

Nick Worrall attributes Meyerhold's interest in the collective synchronization of movement to "the structural discoveries of Cubism."[36] What Edward Fry describes in Cubist painting as a "visual gestalt of the highest possible unity," Worrall describes in Meyerhold's *The Magnificent Cuckold* as a "pattern of interrelatedness,"[37] a unity and cohesiveness beyond that of part to whole; the parts were, in their own autonomous structure and motion, microcosms of the larger pictorial structure. The perceptual areas, like individual planes and volumes in Cubist paintings, transcended their superficial, compartmental status to participate in the pictorial continuum of the stage picture.

For Meyerhold, stage movement was to be organized according to a contrapuntal principle into a plastic unity of actor and scenic properties. This method of a contrapuntal synthesis of the scenic ensemble resembled Léger's idea that "human material may be used in groups moving in a parallel or contrasting rhythms, on the condition that the general effect is in no way sacrificed to it."[38] In effect, both Léger and Meyerhold sought a thorough stylistic and formalistic dialogue of forms between foreground and background.

Meyerhold's mechanical choreography, his *bio-mechanical* movement, contributed to the total stylistic and formal synthesis of the mise-en-scène. When removed from the context of production, the bio-mechanical movements and gestures could theoretically be explained as the application of a mechanical theory to the actor; in practice, however, the actors' movements had an inextricable bond to the set piece and contributed to the integration of geometric forms on stage. It was in this integrative function that movement appeared Cubistic: as foreground elements, movement became formal repetitions and echoes of the patterns in the scaffold. When placed in the context of production, into the Cubistic scheme of the mise-en-scène, the angular, mechanical, and boldly demarcated movements of the actors were seen as paradigmatic extensions of the geometric design of the background.

To secure the integration of individual perceptual areas with the general stage picture, to strengthen the dialogue between elements of the foreground and background, Meyerhold needed a uniform costume that would fit into the architectonic design of the scaffold and give a mechanized, angular, kinetic quality to the actors' movements. He designed a costume that exaggerated the planar architecture of the human anatomy and connected the configurations of movement, gesture, and pose with the architectonic configurations of the set construction.

Meyerhold's actors wore blue overalls, or *prozodezhda* (work or factory clothes), which were actually adaptations of the type of costume worn by actors in *Mystery Bouffe* and *The Dawns.* The seams on these garments were reinforced and turned outward, and the voluminous sections on the upper leg were accentuated. The loose-fitting coverall magnified the architectural construction of the leg, the cylindrical shape of the arms, creating a flattened appearance and, in general, highlighting the structural features of the human anatomy.

Meyerhold reduced movement to an essential, geometric purity: not the form of naturalistic movement but a stylized architectural design that he harmonized with other scenic elements. The architectural, geometric qualities of the *prozodezhda* enhanced the stylized, angular movements of the actors.

The *prozodezhda,* then, gave the human frame the "structural patterning of human figure depiction in Cubist painting."[39] Set in an architectonic shell, moving with a plastic, geometric rigidity, the actor blended perfectly with the architectural framework of the set piece, resembling the fragmented and dispersed planes and volumes in the geometricized foreground and background of Cubist paintings.

The *prozodezhda* functioned "as a sign of a general condition or collective function;"[40]; any additions to the costumes, such as pom-poms, eyeglasses, or riding crop, served as condensed signs of a specific, significant quality of the character. Like Picasso and Braque, Meyerhold gave a geometric treatment to three-dimensional forms, integrating the pictorial field in uniform, stark architectonic shapes.

Meyerhold created a formalistic synthesis, a homogenous landscape of geometric forms fused in space. The stage picture was an architectural synthesis in which all parts had equal strength and were subservient to the general visual gestalt. The costumes, designed to emphasize the geometric configuration of the body, encouraged mechanical, angular movements; the poses and gestures, being echoes and repetitions of one another, linked the various perceptual areas together and to the scaffold, thereby fusing the subject and field together in space.

The homogenous stage picture, like Picasso's *Ma Jolie,* consisted in an expansive linear grid perforated by diagonal vectors; the vectors, in this case, were the lines of the actors' bodies, gestures, group formations, and their spatial placement. These vectors and patterns of actors, in pose and gesture, functioned as dynamic imagery; the imagery interacted with the field, was not set against it, and, like the clef, hand, and lettering in *Ma Jolie,* not only originated in but also precipitated pictorial space. Foreground and background contributed equally as structural components in the continuum of the shallow landscape.

Closing the three-dimensional space by fusing foreground and background into one continuum, Meyerhold made the stage picture plane an "anticlimactic" dialogue of forms; except in those instances where the spotlights isolated a single actor or group—such as Stella with the flower and Bruno's nightmare—no central figure or formation drew attention away from any other area. There was no visual climax on the stage. The stage picture plane was the origin and conclusion of all pictorial elements; it contained an incessant dialogue between surface and depth.

The dialogue between the scenic forms created a dynamic effect or impression in the stage picture. The set was not treated as a static, recessive background to the actors as it had been in Symbolism. The lines of the set, movement, gesture, and costumes were all thoroughly integrated so that their interaction created not only a homogenous stage picture but also a pictorial dynamism through the "anticlimactic" dialogue of geometric shapes.

Giving the production of *The Magnificent Cuckold* a stylized Cubistic pictorial treatment, Meyerhold became vulnerable to the same problem that Picasso and Braque encountered in abstraction; geometric distortion hindered recognition and obscured meaning. The Cubist painters incorporated typographical and realistic elements in the picture surface to make their portrayals comprehensible; these inclusions were specific referents to the subject and were intended to bridge abstraction and cognizance. Meyerhold employed similar devices.

The white letters, CR ML NCK, painted on the black rotating disc were obvious typographical clues, being a distillation of the playwright's name. An additional letter, "X," appeared at four locations on Popova's scaffold: on the front panel of the doors above and below the trestle platform stage right and on the panel of each hinged window on the upper and lower frame of the stage-left scaffold. Whereas the letters CR ML NCK seemed to have a semantic reference, the four Xs had no specific semantic context.

What connected all the letters on the set piece was the fact that they were painted on moving parts: the wheel spun, the two doors revolved, and the two windows opened. The typographical signs on the construction were not specifically used to indicate particular objects, as was the inclusion "JOU" for *journal* in Picasso's *Still-Life With Chair-Caning,* but were employed as signals for functional, mobile parts. Meaning and context evolved not from the semantic connotations of the letters but from the functioning of the parts and the manner in which they were used: Bruno squatting in an open window; the door bumping actors off the platform and onto the slide; the wheel spinning to indicate some emotion or psychologism.

Whenever the doors, windows, or wheel moved, their movement was noticed, or emphasized, because they were the only inscribed parts on the scaffold. That each part moved brought attention to its function, and the function to the context in which that part was used. The context established, in turn, the meaning or identity of the part. Once an identity had been determined, the part took on literal significance and became, through its functioning, a realistic clue in the abstract field. The revolving door, for example, when passed through, functioned simply as a gate or other mobile barrier between two areas; when used as an instrument for batting unwelcome characters, it obviously acted as a weapon. The distortion brought about by abstracting the set piece was somewhat clarified through the functioning of the practicable parts.

Meyerhold introduced other, more obvious, literal clues to give sense and context to the abstract landscape. Some of these have already been mentioned as condensed signs: the set of rotating wooden sails signified the mill; the flower in Stella's hand signified a terrace, and the pom-poms around Bruno's neck a childish demeanor. Other props and costumes had the same effect, supplying what Nick Worrall calls "sign systems"; these include "riding gaiters for the Count worn over his overalls, the appropriate hat and badge of office for the burgomaster, a quill pen for Estrugo the clerk, etc."[41] In addition, there were caps, cloaks, and rifles for the militia and dark aprons for the women of the village.

These items served the same function as Braque's realistically painted nail in *Still-Life With Violin and Pitcher*. As realistic referents inside a complex pattern of interlocking and uniform planes, they bridged the abstract and concrete, providing memory-images by which the spectator could reconstruct the subject. Meyerhold's mise-en-scène, like some Cubist paintings, contained "the scheme of forms and small real details as stimuli integrated into the unity of the work"[42] so that the spectator could assimilate the scenographic data into a finished, intelligible structure.

Meyerhold's production of *The Magnificent Cuckold* and Cubist painting had similar effects: Each actively engaged the viewer in the work of art through an act of the imagination. An expenditure of the imagination was needed to analyze the fragmented subject, study the anatomy of the new form, and discern its meaning. The stage, like the painting, was a vehicle for created meanings, open perspectives, and a shared creative effort on the part of the artist and spectator.

The Death of Tarelkin (1922)

Meyerhold originally staged Alexander Sukhovo-Kobylin's "satire of tsarist police methods"[43] in October 1917, at the Alexandrinsky Theatre in Petersburg. On November 24, 1922, he staged a new version of *The Death of*

Tarelkin in Moscow, where the play joined the repertoire with *The Magnificent Cuckold* at the Actor's Theatre, then a subsidiary of the State Institute of Theatrical Art.

The Death of Tarelkin has been categorized as an example of *Eccentricism*, a theatrical style of the early twenties that made extensive use of circus devices. Nikolai Gorchakov believed that the staging of *Tarelkin* was stylistically similar to Meyerhold's staging of *The Magnificent Cuckold* because the relationship of actors to construction in both productions resembled that of circus performers to circus instruments or machines.[44] *Tarelkin* and *Cuckold* contained utilitarian machines for acting, stage properties and constructions that could either be manipulated or manipulate. Meyerhold's young actors, many of them still students, needed the dexterity and precision of circus acrobats and clowns to handle successfully the circus-like contraptions designed by Meyerhold and Varvara Stepanova.

On a bare, brightly lit stage stood several wooden apparati, all painted white and devoid of ornamentation. The series of individual machines and pieces of mechanized furniture replaced the single free-standing scaffold of *Cuckold* but retained the potential for supporting and interacting with the actors; Meyerhold designed these "acting instruments" so that they could be "shifted and used by the actors as required."[45] Each device concealed a functional gimmick, a trap, that was put into play by the actors. A chair, for example, had a spring-loaded seat which, when sat on, would collapse and deposit the actor on the floor; a blank cartridge would explode when an actor sat on a certain stool. The police torture chamber and prison consisted of a single low platform with an enormous grinder and latticed cage; prisoners were led up a ladder, dropped head first into the mouth of a chimney, then ground through a rotating wheel and spat out into the latticed cell.

These devices, like the scaffold for *Cuckold,* were not totally representational. They were anchored to representational functions first by their appearance and, secondly, by their practicability. It was through functioning that the machines became specific objects.

Stepanova costumed the actors in loose-fitting overalls decorated with stripes, rectangular patches, and other linear patterns so as to suggest a convict's uniform. Striped caps and gaiters were worn by some actors. The costumes quartered the body into either planer or cylindrical lozenges with bold demarcations between the different areas. The linear markings on the costumes and the geometric shapes created by these markings repeated the shapes in the furniture and apparatus.

Judging from these descriptions, it is obvious that the acting machines and the costumes presented caricatures of real objects. Nothing was so totally abstract that sense or context disappeared; rather, the stage objects seemed to be exaggerations, iconic hyperboles, of real objects. This same sort of exaggeration Meyerhold gave to his characters, instructing them to employ "once again the knockabout tricks of circus clowns and strolling players."[46]

The actor in Meyerhold's theatre functioned as a go-between for the production aesthetics and the play; the audience was first to recognize the performer, then, through the performance, the play. The actors' responsibility was to develop scenic situations in which the core of the situation was revealed; the "actor-tribune" was not to act the situation per se, "but what [was] concealed behind it and what it [had] to reveal for a specifically propagandist purpose."[47] The role presented not a person but an *image* of some concept, and the performance was a reduction of the concept to an appropriate iconic presentation. In this sense, Meyerhold's actors were grotesque exaggerations of real characters just as Cubist forms were iconic exaggerations of the architecture of real objects.

Just as tricks were built into the machines and other props, the actors were given gimmicks which were intended to strengthen the caricature-like quality of their performances. An actor, in one moment, would be playing the character's emotions or sentiments with sincerity; a second later, he would quickly drop out of character or assume a new attitude. Edward Braun reports one such moment in his book, *Meyerhold on Theatre:*

> Tarelkin, bound hand and foot in prison and frantic with thirst, tried in vain to reach a cup of water held by a warden—then suddenly he winked broadly at the audience and took a long draught from a bottle of wine he had concealed in his pocket.[48]

Other tricks by actors were inserted into Meyerhold's imaginative production: a thin, young, male actor, without makeup and stuffed with enormous padding under his skirts, played an aging, pregnant washerwoman; assistant directors were planted in the front row of the auditorium and instructed to stand at breaks, fire a blank pistol into the audience, then shout "'Entrrrr-act!'"[49]

The quick change from one attitude to another and the many absurd antics were not written into Sukhovo-Kobylin's script; rather, they were gimmicks Meyerhold devised to put a distance between the actors and their characters, to exaggerate the thematic core of the script, and to demonstrate the fictitious reality of the performance.

While Meyerhold gave a more thorough Cubistic treatment to *The Magnificent Cuckold,* there were several rather obvious Cubist elements he carried over to *The Death of Tarelkin.* The application of a Cubist aesthetics was more general, here widely dispersed in small degrees through several aspects of the production.

Perhaps the most obvious Cubistic feature in the *Tarelkin* production was the architectonic basis in the composition of foreground and background elements. The Cubist painters perfected the formal elements of their paintings by exaggerating and abstracting the most basic structural characteristics of the subjects; this produced an intellectualization of the underlying architecture, a suggestion of the subject. Planted in the Cubistic composition were recognizable forms and shapes to orient the viewer.

Meyerhold's machines for acting, likewise, depicted the subject through the exaggeration and abstraction of its essential architecture, creating a suggestion of a recognizable object. In the distribution of internal salient forms and in its functioning, the machine for acting produced an intelligible description of the object it was to represent. The prison, for example, was not only suggested by the vertical slats on the latticed cage, indicating bars, but also by the chute and enormous rotating wheel, the meat-grinder for reforming convicts.

In the same way, Stepanova's costumes became intelligible. The stripes and geometric patches on the overalls and caps were reminiscent of the linear, striped patterns on convicts' uniforms.

Meyerhold's approach to designing the scenographic elements in *Tarelkin* resembled the approach the Cubist painters employed to portray their subjects' abstraction: faceting internal forms and function in the interest of a conceived visual logic and "the necessity of describing the subject."[50] Here, as in *Cuckold,* the set pieces and props did not strictly conform to the nonrepresentational function normally associated with Constructivist staging. In the theatrical context, the objects needed to assume a specific identity, and this was accomplished in a Cubistic way: in the reduction of real appearances to recognizable geometric forms and through specific and thematic functioning.

The Cubists achieved homogeneity in their paintings by distributing familial forms and volumes in space. Stepanova and Meyerhold created a harmonious, homogenous stage picture in much the same way. Constructing the apparatus and costumes in geometric, linear patterns, accentuating internal architectonic features, then juxtaposing them in space, they created a visual fusion of form and line. The broad vertical stripes on the overalls and caps repeated the vertical striping in the positive and negative planes of the grinder and cell; the rectangles, triangles, squares, and horizontal stripes on the other costumes corresponded visually to the square chimney, the negative triangular plane in the space between the leaning ladder and chimney, the horizontal steps on the ladder, the horizontal side bars on the cell, and the angular features of the furniture.

The homogeneity of familial forms distributed in space gave the mise-en-scène a formalistic resemblance to the picture surface in Synthetic

Cubism. Meyerhold and Stepanova integrated the apparatus and costumes into plastic environs by rendering stage properties in simple geometrical shapes, in underlying objective forms that seemed to be sculpted and free-standing in space; this heightened the sculptural presence of the forms on stage.

Unlike the pictorial effect in *Cuckold,* in which the sensation of three-dimensionality and sculptural illusion were subordinated to the homogenous anticlimactic landscape, the stage picture in *Tarelkin,* like Synthetic Cubist paintings, projected a sculptural presence through distancing; the constructions and costumes seemed to press outward from the pictorial space. The surface/depth dialogue of *Cuckold* was here severely curtailed; the sculpted objects were closed by strong boundaries and contours to accentuate the distance between them.

The difference between the geometric markings on the costumes and the lines of the apparatus and furniture was great enough to set one object off from another; an impression of depth and distance between objects was created. The actors and free-standing constructions were essentially paradigmatic fragments dispersed over the stage picture plane, but they did not build a landscape in the way that the actor and scaffold did in *Cuckold.* The objects in the pictorial field were autonomous, sculpted markings situated at random in space, in depth, despite their plastic appearances.

The paradigmatic forms overlapped, like the objects in Synthetic Cubism, retaining their shape and solidity, their anatomical autonomy, and created bold contrasts of form, line, and texture on the picture plane. Actors did not blend into the prison cell when standing in front of it, despite the vertical stripes that connected them visually; the apparatus and costumes were autonomous forms placed on a common field at a distance from one another. The same was true of the furniture: it did not disappear into the background but was an independent paradigmatic element placed at a distance from similar objects in space.

The level of abstraction in the stage picture was consequently reduced, as it had been in Synthetic Cubism, and, as the separation between forms and objects became noticeable, content became more comprehensible. In *Harlequin* (1915), Picasso dehumanized the human figure by composing it in three slightly tilted, rectangular planes placed one behind the other. Tilted to the right, the front panel was painted with crosshatching lines and diamonds to depict the harlequin's costume. Tilted to the left, the second panel put a distance between the first and the last. The third panel, tilted to the right, constituted the trunk, head, and skull of the figure. It was the similarity of the rectangular forms and the distance between them that made the subject recognizable, the middle panel bisecting the body and giving the viewer room to reconstruct the dispersed image. The solid area around the figure set it off, accentuating its architectural, sculptural presence and its autonomous identity in the field.

Meyerhold's machines for acting did not need to function in order to define themselves. Each had sufficient space around it so that its identity was obvious. Even the four separate parts of the prison (i.e., ladder, chimney, grinder, and cell), which were built onto one narrow platform, were differentiated by the space around them: The ladder leaned into and connected with the chimney but was separated by the space between its frame and the body of the chimney; connected to the grinder, the chimney was separated by the contrast between the rigid line of its shell and the circumference of the grinder and by its height; the cage was linked to the grinder but appeared separate as a result of its squareness when juxtaposed with the round wheel. Stepanova, like Picasso, made an abstract object recognizable by putting both an actual and a formalistic distance between each of the individual planes of the image. Other objects became intelligible in the same way: familial forms sculpted and separated in and by space.

Although James Symons claimed that the production of *Tarelkin* "was all pretty much what the audiences had seen in *The Magnificent Cuckold*,"[51] photographs of the production showed that Meyerhold was more interested in grouping his actors into thematic gestalts than purely visual gestalts. Certainly, the arrangement of actors on the set of *Tarelkin* was governed by a concern for independent perceptual areas: the two actors with raised fists constituted one area, the standing actor a second area, the seated actor a third, and so on. Highly sculpted and independent images, these separate areas did not, however, act as independent visual nuclei. The eye could not rest on a single group or individual and find it visually informational; it was necessary to refer to the other areas to decipher the meaning or significance of any one area. The actors with raised fists had interest only in that they participated in the sequence of four actors as indices of aggression or violence. This attitude of aggression was continued in the standing actor who appeared in a threatening pose beside the seated actor. What made this scene visually interesting was the thematic information, the aggression, passed from one perceptual area to another.

Although each was an independent plastic image, the logic of the individual areas did not emerge from the purely visual pattern, as it did in *Cuckold,* but from the thematic inference seen informationally across the stage picture plane. The stage picture seemed to have one thematic and pictorial nucleus in the manner of illusionism, and that nucleus informed the entire composition despite the several perceptual areas arranged plastically in space.

Perhaps the organization of actors into perceptual areas with thematic/visual motives followed the example of Synthetic Cubism. In both

Harlequin and *The Card Player,* Picasso divided the picture plane into areas of specific reference which, when joined in the imagination, participated in the thematic import of the painting. The level of abstraction had been reduced by making objects more recognizable, preserving contours and shape to establish thematic relationships, and building theme through self-explanatory references. This much was certainly evident in *Tarelkin.* Some of the props and furniture could be used in several ways, in more than one context: the chair functioned as a spring-loaded seat, a stool acted as a pistol, depending on how it was used. The prop was manipulated in this production as whole areas of the scaffold were used in *Cuckold:* the function of the stage object was not restricted by form, by realistic references; the object had a variable, fluctuating content, a transmutable meaning.

The prison structure and costumes have already been described as iconic caricatures of real objects. Caricatures and plastic pictorial forms in the stage picture, the apparatus and costumes contained the primary attributes of their realistic equivalents and functioned as condensed signs. The prison was, in a sense, a refinery: convicts were fed into it, ground up, "refined," then boxed in a cell. The apparatus contained the machinery for all these functions. The stage construction was a synthesis of both form and function, a plastic, objective fusion of form and content.

The condensed sign, apart from its operational identity, also functioned as an independent visual form. The condensed signs Picasso incorporated in *The Three Musicians* (i.e., a cylinder and black circle to depict a clarinet) were at once referents to real objects and autonomous pictorial elements.

This was also the case with Stepanova's various apparati. They could be seen, on one hand, as abstract, condensed signs and, at the same time, as self-sufficient sculpted forms in the pictorial space of the stage: the prison an assemblage of two leaning parallel lines, a box, a sphere, and a latticed, upright rectangle. The prison, like Cubistic condensed signs, created itself as an object, as an independent visual form.

Closely aligned to the notion of condensed sign was the concept *tableau-object,* or the *painting-as-object.* Cubist paintings had nonillusionistic value in that they made no attempt to reproduce reality. The paintings were not to be seen as mirrors to nature but as natural objects in their own right; objects participating in reality, they had a character, a personality, of their own.

Meyerhold gave many of his props this same quality. They were not only to be manipulated by actors but were to manipulate in return. In this way, they became personified and took on a unique character. When the prop or set displayed faculties and behavior normally attributed to humans, such as emotion or reason, and acted independently of the actor, it became something greater than a condensed sign; it became *prop-as-character.*

This device was obviously employed by Meyerhold in *The Magnificent Cuckold,* where, for example, the scaffold spun its wheels and discs to comment on the action or reveal a psychologism. It was used far more extensively in *Tarelkin.* Not only would the prison apparatus swallow and digest convicts, but many of the other trick-loaded acting machines behaved independently as well: chairs and stools bucked occupants and fired missiles; legs of tables gave way. In each case, the prop-as-character became a personality with its own distinctive motives.

Although *The Death of Tarelkin* followed on the success of *The Magnificent Cuckold,* it was not received with the same enthusiasm and praise. Not only was Sukhovo-Kobylin's satire outdated and inappropriate to a burlesque treatment, but Meyerhold encountered several technical problems during the production. The acting machines would frequently malfunction; the loose-fitting overalls obscured the actors' stylized movements, and the searchlights at the front of the auditorium would often dim, leaving the actors in semi-darkness.

Whether these difficulties disappointed Meyerhold and triggered the radical stylistic changes in subsequent productions is a matter of conjecture. James Symons believes that Meyerhold confronted the problems in *Tarelkin* and "began to modify what he himself called, 'the stylistic extremes' of '*Cuckold*' and '*Tarelkin*'."[52] For whatever reasons, Meyerhold's productions after *Tarelkin* took a slight turn toward conservatism. This turn left behind the obvious, blatant display of Cubist influence. What Cubist elements did appear were presented in more subtle ways and with less visual impact.

The Forest (1924)

Cubism embodied a preference on the part of the painters for a conceived reality over a perceived reality. Picasso said, "I paint objects as I think them, not as I see them."[53] Searching for a new compositional order, an architectonic basis, the Cubists exaggerated underlying geometric forms of real objects. Through geometricization, the anatomy of the object was fragmented into central shapes, then dispersed by an invented logic.

Meyerhold's method for staging plays resembled the Cubists' approach to painting. Meyerhold explained, "'I,' my personal attitude to life, precedes all else. Everything which I take as material for my art corresponds not to the truth of reality but to the truth of my personal artistic whim."[54]

Meyerhold searched for a new compositional order by which to organize a production, and he, too, discovered that geometricization was

· an appropriate and effective method. Just as the Cubists broke actual objects into fragments of underlying, essential forms or blocks, Meyerhold reduced the playscript to a series of fragments, or episodes, he felt were central to the thought of the author and, consequently, to a production. The play contained the central *idea* around which all aspects of the staging were to be arranged.

Meyerhold and the Cubists loathed traditional "artistic" conventions. Meyerhold believed that the unities of time, place, and action forced on the director an unacceptable and restrictive division of the play into a linear, sequential, cause and effect progression of acts. The play, he thought, needed a division by episodes so that the idea of the play, and the idea of each episode, could be given emphasis.

Meyerhold devised a number of ways to underline the central idea of the episodes. He would often give each scene its own title or play each episode as a separate scene, setting it off with pauses, music, or different decors. At other times, Meyerhold would run the episodes together, creating a pattern of overlapping individual actions. These methods had painterly counterparts in Cubism: closed planar construction in which the composition was made up of solid, differentiated fragments and its open planar structure in which fragments opened at the contours, producing a field of integrated, overlapping forms. Meyerhold and the Cubists fragmented the subject to present its central idea, its basic form, in a pattern of integrated fragments or episodes.

The painters did not see the object as a complete entity; they were concerned with the object as an interaction of many innate forms and shapes that, when abstracted and juxtaposed, described the object. Meyerhold's notion of montage echoed this Cubist concern. Montage was, for Meyerhold, a system of episodic contrasts, "a conflict of episodes."[55] Whenever any two elements were juxtaposed, a correlation emerged in the mind of the viewer; the correlation, in turn, produced an intelligible portrayal. This was the nature of cinematic montage, which Meyerhold adapted to stage presentations. "My production of *The Forest* was constructed on exactly the same principle, on the conflict of episodes."[56]

Meyerhold divided Ostrovsky's five-act play into thirty-three episodes. He ignored the original thematic sequence, placing the episodes in an invented order that he felt would highlight the satirical aspect of the play, and arranged the scenes so that they cut back and forth between two simultaneous stories. Meyerhold reordered scenes, played two or more scenes simultaneously, and altered the locales of several episodes, all in an effort to magnify certain central actions of Ostrovsky's play.

Dismantling the five acts, Meyerhold then searched for the most characteristic mode of expression for each of the thirty-three episodes.

Although he changed little of Ostrovsky's dialogue, he ignored its meaning and invented action and scenes on the basis of the images and words in the text. When a pair of lovers, for example, were planning an elopement, their dialogue was synchronized with the back and forth motion of the swing they sat on; their rising elation was indicated by an increased momentum in their swinging. When brooding over her servitude, a washerwoman thrashed the laundry as a demonstration of her contempt for her employer; "a flood of furs, shoes, and hats [dropped] down on the stage from above"[57] when a merchant swore to forego his property. In each episode, the central motive or idea was magnified through the action; the action became an objective signal of the structural basis of the scene.

These episodic variations on Ostrovsky's text were the structural basis of the production. The episodes, presented either singularly or simultaneously, were introduced by titles projected onto a screen. Characters appeared, gradually advancing the theme through the episode, and each episode magnified essential structural points or nuclei in the playscript. The production, then, was constructed like a Cubist painting: a number of individual fragments were placed against or on top of one another in an ascending and invented sequential order; their spatial and temporal arrangement eventually described the subject — presented the story — through an associational process. As the Cubists "cubified" the anatomy of actual objects, Meyerhold "cubified" the anatomy of Ostrovsky's text through episodic fragmentation. In both media, the objective was the same: to portray the subject in an assemblage, a montage, of familial architectonic units.

Meyerhold designed a simplistic and sparse scenography, one that was flexible enough to present the rapid sequence of episodes in any order or method he desired. Neutral curtains flanked the sides of the stage, leaving the back brick wall exposed. The stage was practically bare except for a long and narrow spiral wooden ramp that was suspended from the flies. This ramp, which was labeled "a bridge road,"[58] stood fifteen feet above the ground at its highest point upstage center, descended across the stage-right area and terminated at the center of the orchestra pit. There were, in addition, ladders and a skeletal, latticed trellis on stage, but most of the action took place on the bare stage floor and the suspended structure. Meyerhold dispersed the action through a number of impermanent, individual locales to facilitate the quick and continuous changes of episodes. "The stage and its spaces resembled the interior of a kinema studio, and the whole thing suggested a first attempt at transferring kinematographic movement, variety and speed to the stage."[59]

Actors brought onto the bare stage realistic props and real objects that were to be utilized in unusual ways. These objects were not restricted to their literal or realistic value: "a table might be used as a bridge, a chair as a knoll, and so on. . . ."⁶⁰ The real objects, like the abstract constructions and apparatus in *Cuckold,* had an open, flexible content; their real form did not regulate or restrict their usage.

The actors transformed the bare stage space into specific locales by manipulating the objects:

> The transformation of the neutral constructional equipment and its separate parts [took] place continuously during the whole show. The actor [changed], by his enactment, the very meaning and significance of these constructions and apparatuses. . . . The park bench placed behind a trellis in the rendezvous episode, or a table and a chair and bell placed behind the same trellis in the episode "The Piqued Dame" give a different meaning to the semi-circular matted wall; in the first case it becomes a bower in the orchard, in the second, the boudoir of Gourmishsky.⁶¹

The actor, then, through his action on the properties and neutral areas created the scenic environment, making the stage an open and variable space.

The open content of the props and the variable aspect of the playing area corresponded to the nature of form and pictorial field in Cubism. The stage in Meyerhold's production was not restricted by traditional unities or naturalistic procedures; its flexible, chameleonic substance enabled Meyerhold to shape and transform it at will, to fracture it into a number of independent, seemingly unrelated planes of content. The spiraling ramp represented a bridge, a forest, and an attic in defiance of any naturalistic convention.

Just as the Cubist painters rendered objects in simultaneous viewpoints over a single pictorial surface, Meyerhold played several scenes simultaneously in one scenic field: the travelling players Arkashka and Gennady gradually meandered down the spiraling catwalk from episode to episode; their leisurely pace seemed out of synch with the frenzy in the domestic scene below as they leisurely cast their rods over the side of the bridge; and, at other moments, Meyerhold lit single scenes, giving them emphasis in their isolation and projecting descriptive titles on the screen or rear wall. The stage picture had the same elasticity that Cubism had: restrictions on time and place in Meyerhold's production and on form and content in Cubism were disregarded. The associational faculties of the spectator's imagination pulled the episodes and scenes together in the same way the mind organized fragmented and simultaneous Cubist portrayals.

Meyerhold employed a system of signs in *The Forest* similar to that in *Cuckold.* An abstract and elastic architecture served as a backdrop for properties that made specific references depending on how they were used. The ability of objects to become specific referents derived from their elastic qualities, from their role as transmutable meaning and condensed sign. A plain wood chair acted as a knoll and a podium, being variously transformed by the actor; the trellis assumed a specific identity when used as a piece of garden furniture for it projected all the atmospheric associations of a pastoral scene.

The objects in *The Forest* displayed an additional sign function, one similar to the object sign function in Picasso's *Still-Life With Fringe*. William Tucker claims that the balls of fringe dangling from the protruding shelf play a specific symbolic role: "there dangles the fringe, the motif and colour of which recall the heavily decorated gold frames enclosing Old Master paintings."[62] There is more than a purely utilitarian sign function to the ornamental fringe that dangles off the shelf; the fringe is more than a shelf cover. According to Tucker, the fringe refers specifically to a school of painting and to an actual object; these references are immediately recognized despite the fact that the fringe is accompanied by everyday items, such as a knife and a piece of bread, in an alogical, sculpted assemblage. The gold fringe functions as a symbol of a style (i.e., Old Master paintings) and a specific historical context.

Meyerhold's use of costumes, props, and special effects, all placed in an abstract architectural setting, had a pointed, connotative function similar to that of objects in Cubism. Meyerhold dressed one young, voluptuous woman in a gaudy pink gown and applied her makeup naturalistically; a second woman dressed in an identical manner except that she wore an emerald green wig. Apparently, both women wore gowns indicative of nineteenth-century dress, supplying a strong contrast to the young boy who wore tennis shorts and a white shirt.

This same contrast of styles appeared again in the stage properties. Meyerhold placed a chair and footstool of nineteenth-century design alongside several plain, ordinary wooden chairs. The props, like the costumes, acted as precise referents to a specific period; their specificity within a nonrepresentational setting gave them the same symbolic value as the gold fringe in Picasso's *Still-Life With Fringe*.

Other properties and effects were employed as emblematic or symbolic referents. The shower of furs, shoes, and hats was emblematic of a character's mercantile trade; an actress playing a washerwoman thrashed the clothes that were emblems of her servitude; an actor playing an enterprising and deceitful speculator dressed as Satan, and his disciple produced thunder by rattling a sheet of tin.

In these examples, the objects and effects had no general contextual value inside the sparse setting; they did not contribute to a larger scene or atmosphere. They functioned as either emblems or symbols, as signs, of specific situations, identities, or moods. Their placement in an alogical context, like the fringe in the assemblage of ordinary objects, increased their referential power. "The single object [was] thus invested with the concentrated essence of its time and [stamped] its impressions forcibly on our memories."[63]

Give Us Europe (1924)

Meyerhold staged *Give Us Europe* in 1924 at the Meyerhold Theatre in Moscow. The agit-prop production was an adaptation of Ilya Ehrenburg's novel, *The Give-Us-Europe Trust*, about the struggle between American capitalists and The Trust, a Soviet radio network, for control of Europe. Gorchakov claims that, although the novel served as the primary source for the production, the playscript was actually a compilation of extracts from novels by Hamp, Kellerman, Ehrenburg, and Upton Sinclair.[64]

As with *The Forest*, Meyerhold built the production on a series of episodes. The production has frequently been described as a political revue in seventeen episodes. Forty-five actors performed more than ninety roles but rarely did a single character appear in more than one episode. The rapid sequence of scenes contributed to the montage format for the production.

James Symons believes that with this production Meyerhold wanted to "mobilize" the staging, hoping to create a production technique comparable to the mobility his actors acquired through bio-mechanics.[65] In addition to fragmenting the action into episodes, Meyerhold devised other means to create a sensation of rapid and continuous motion in the stage picture. These included projections on three screens, spotlighting either to illuminate single areas or to weave quickly over the stage, and a highly flexible, transmutable setting.

Meyerhold's dynamic setting for *Give Us Europe* was an extension of his increasing interest in bringing cinematic devices to the theatre. He and his designer, Ilya Shlepyanov, designed a system of moving walls, each of the eight to ten red wooden panels measuring approximately twelve feet long and nine feet high; mounted on wheels, the walls were moved around the stage by stagehands concealed behind each screen. They moved either singularly or in combinations to present a number of locations:

> They permitted the place of action to be shifted rapidly. A lecture hall was quickly transformed into a street with an endless fence. The street then became a chamber of parliament.[66]

The mobile walls were made of slats of wood and were placed either on end or side; they acted primarily as backdrops to the action and other props. Tables, chairs, desks, and other real objects were placed in front of the screens. Other objects were hung by wires from the top edge of a screen to lend even greater specificity to the scene.

Apart from their scenic function, the walls also became characters, or at least active, animated objects, during the performance. They operated as though they possessed their own will and motivation, displaying actions that were appropriate and timely to the thin plot. Braun describes a scene in which a fugitive fled upstage only to disappear between two screens; converging on the actor, who squeezed between them, the walls seemed to swallow the fugitive, for when they parted again, the actor had disappeared; unseen, he slipped off stage behind one of the moving panels. Gorchakov describes a chase scene, perhaps the same described by Braun, in which the "spotlights rushed about chaotically and suddenly all the panels began twirling around in different directions."[67] It is obvious that the walls, in these instances, were not functioning as mere backgrounds but acting as vehicles whose roles were defined by their actions.

Meyerhold projected slides onto screens placed around and above the stage. The projections carried titles and locations of each episode as well as comments on the characters and action. Quotations from the literature and speeches of Russian statesmen such as Lenin and Trotsky were also projected on the screens.

The end of all these innovative devices was to create a dynamic stage picture. The rapid scene changes, the quick and frequent changes of characters, the episodic revue structure, the kinetic constructions, whirling lights, and flickering projections all gave the action on stage a dynamic, pulsating mobile quality "of almost motion-picturelike impetuosity."[68]

Meyerhold's production of *Give Us Europe* possessed the dynamic sensation which Jean Metzinger ascribed to Picasso's paintings. Writing in the Parisian journal, *Pan,* October 1910, Metzinger claimed that Picasso gave his paintings "a free mobile perspective." The sensation of movement in Cubist painting was achieved by exaggerating the staccato rhythm in the interaction of architectonic forms, producing a mechanized, clockwork energy. Picasso painted the subject in small disjointed images; these disjointed units created an inorganic, mechanized assembly of geometric forms that were actually exaggerated architectonic features of the subject. These small fragments were then joined in rapid succession to produce a semblance of cinematographic movement on the surface of the painting. At every point on the picture plane, the image was likely to change quickly; the perspective became a scattered, abrupt juxtaposition of architectonic units.

Meyerhold organized this revue in an identical fashion. The episodes were architectonic units of the production and contained only what was essential to the theme or plot. Characters, for example, were divided into two groups: the bourgeois and the Soviet socialists. The former were re-hearsed in a grotesque, flamboyant behavior to exaggerate their hideous and superfluous vices; the heroes, the Soviet proletariat, behaved in a more realistic fashion, judicious, virtuous, and responsible. Capitalist debauchery was presented in one scene by a chorus line of attractive women dressed in black mesh stockings and tights and dancing to a spirited jazz score. The proletariat, on the other hand, was depicted as "good, clean, upright..."[69] As the Cubists reduced real objects to their most essential and exaggerated architectonic shapes, Meyerhold pared the episodes to a single, exaggerated characteristic action.

Building the performance in seventeen episodes with more than ninety roles, or caricatures, Meyerhold made the production a revue montage of small disjointed units of the story line. The many scenes and episodes were juxtaposed in rapid succession; a staccato rhythm developed from the abrupt interaction of one scene and episode with another and from the several devices Meyerhold used to create dynamism in the production.

Given the quick scene changes, the lamps lighting in rapid alternate turns, different scenes at different locations on the stage, and the contin-uous array of characters-as-images, the stage picture resembled a montage of frames on celluloid; this effect was repeated in the quickly changing slide projections. There was a scattered abrupt juxtaposition of scenes and episodes, creating the same "free, mobile perspective" that characterized Cubist paintings.

The mobile perspective in Cubism resulted from the abrupt juxtaposi-tion of plastic units and, in the late Analytic phase, of open planar struc-tures. Once Picasso and Braque tore open the bold contours of the geometric shapes in the early Analytic phase, they produced an abstract portrayal in which the features of the subject melted into one another; the planes that were once closed suddenly opened and merged into one another. This tech-nique created a fluid iconography in which planes easily and almost imper-ceptibly dissolved into neighboring areas. Realistically rendered forms eliminated the ensuing confusion, as did typographical elements and either real objects or simulations of real objects.

Meyerhold's ingenious use of the mobile walls produced the same effect on stage that open planar structure created in Cubism. The panels were rectangles, objective only in their nondescript plasticity and geo-metry, and took their identity from the stage action associated with them. Their content was not fixed by their form, and as they shifted across the stage, indicating shifts in locale, they created a pattern of merging planes of location and action. The scenes, in this way, did not end abruptly with blackouts or character changes but dissolved into one another as the mobile panels shifted across the stage; the result was a network of open planes of action created by the movement of the red wooden screens. Each plane was integrated — in the manner of the open, merging planes in Cubist paintings — by the subject, or theme, of the stage action.

Meyerhold risked the danger of completely abstracting the subject and, following the example of Cubist artists, placed precise referents inside the abstract mixture of open planes in order to describe the scene and action. In one scene, five screens were placed in different positions on the stage. Placed in front of, or near, three screens were real objects: a chair and a small desk; a chair and a table covered with a tablecloth; two chairs facing what appeared to be a blackboard or mirror suspended by wires from the top edge of the screen. Three specific locales were simultaneously presented here, in the proximity of real objects to the dispersed screens. The desk and chair suggested an office; the covered table resembled an interior scene in a house; the chairs and blackboard suggested an educational site of some type.

The two remaining screens were placed parallel to each other and the proscenium opening. They were staggered so that the front wall jutted from the stage-left wing onto the playing area, and the right edge of the rear screen continued toward center stage. The two screens looked like walls bordering a narrow street, and it is possible that this arrangement was used for a Moscow street scene. Just as the Cubists indicated specific locales or contexts by placing realistic details of objects in the field of geometric forms, Meyerhold juxtaposed real objects with the rectilinear screens to establish particular locations.

Meyerhold also used titles and descriptions to reduce abstraction. It has been noted that among the projections were titles, passages from speeches, and information on characters and action. These projections functioned as typographical elements in Cubist paintings. They were inserted on the stage picture to make precise references about locale and to define the relationship of one object to another; they established a context in which objects, action, and stage space were to be viewed.

Meyerhold's mobile walls functioned collectively as a means to *create* meanings and context; it was a means used by the Cubists as well. The object in a Cubist painting, by virtue of its open content, ceased to be imitative; Cubism embodied meaning "in forms that create rather than reflect, become rather than describe their subject."[70] Cubist painters were able to reduce real objects through condensed signs to one synthesized, conventional, and characteristic new form.

Mounted on wheels, pushed over the stage by hidden stagehands, the screens were nothing but mobile, planar forms in space, receiving their significance from the action associated with them. The walls were a free, rectangular form with open content; their rectangular, non-literal design enabled them to represent whatever scene was necessary to the action because their rectangularity was a conventional and highly characteristic, almost universal form for any number of interior and exterior objects. Being mobile stage props, the screens were not only part of a dynamic stage picture but, by virtue of their dynamism and versatility, always capable of *becoming* something.

When the screens took on "personalities" of their own—when mobilized by concealed stagehands—they resembled another Cubist device, one closely aligned to condensed signs: tableau-object. As in *The Death of Tarelkin,* the props, the walls, seemed to act at times by their own motivation, to become independent animated forces with their own characters. Related to the idea that a painting was an independent object in reality— not a reproduction or representation of reality—the animated walls became props-as-characters acting side by side with their human counterparts.

Meyerhold's theatre, particularly *Cuckold, Tarelkin,* and *Give Us Europe,* extended form well beyond its literal significance. "The meaning of a place, or an object, became linked intrinsically with human activity, with the creation of meanings in a theatrical landscape...."[71] Momentarily fixed and defined, the open and fluctuating content of the object permitted flexibility of meaning, giving Meyerhold's productions their tremendous versatility. It was Meyerhold's belief that "when...form triumphs over content, then the soul of the theatre will be one."[72]

Treating the mobile panels as condensed signs, employing selective lighting, Meyerhold presented several scenes simultaneously. Connected by theme or plot, the separate scenes appeared as different aspects of the same subject and were dispersed across the stage in the way that the Cubists dispersed various anatomical features of one subject over the picture plane. Separated in space by positive and negative planes—the screens being positive planes and the spaces between them the negative planes—the episodes were tied together in the way the Cubists portrayed the subject in their paintings: through the assimilation of realistic and typographical items and through memory images stored compartmentally in the imagination, then informationally grouped together by association.

There was one other similarity between the appearance of Cubist paintings and the production *Give Us Europe.* In Synthetic Cubism, Picasso and Braque presented the subject in large, geometric planar forms, primarily rectangles; the forms were arranged as planes placed one on top of the other, then painted in bold contrasting colors to distinguish one form or area from another. Into this field of flattened, staggered, rectangular forms, the Cubists placed real objects, quasi-representational renderings, or simulated materials.

Meyerhold's set for *Give Us Europe* projected a picture similar to that of Synthetic Cubism. An enormous back curtain hung from the ceiling and stretched about three quarters of the way across the stage. Where this curtain ended, just right of stage center, a taller, rectangular white panel continued the rest of the way to the stage-right wing. The rectangular projection screen hung from the flies above center stage. This series of curtains and screens created a flattened rectangular background for the other props on stage. The different dimensions of the various rectangular forms accentuated the distance between them without destroying the flattened appearance of the background.

The red wooden mobile walls and other two projection screens were rectangular forms on the stage picture surface. When placed one in front of the other or beside one another, they, too produced a flattened picture, although the distance between them was noticeable. Even when placed diagonally to the rear wall, these props appeared like the planes tilted in opposite directions in Picasso's *The Card Player*.

In addition, the red panels, when viewed as miniscule forms, resembled pieces of wood; when placed either on their sides or ends, the screens became to the stage picture what wood-graining was to Cubist collage. The lines between the slats ran either horizontally or vertically, bringing to the stage picture both a simulation of wood-graining and a strong element of texture. Add the real objects and projections, and Meyerhold's stage picture bore a strong resemblance to Synthetic Cubism: real or realistically drawn forms and typographical elements set in a flattened field of staggered rectangles.

5

Alexander Tairov: Cubistic Productions

Alexander Tairov

In September 1905, Alexander Tairov joined the company at the Komis-sarzhevskaya Theatre in St. Petersburg, where, during the season, he acted in two productions directed by Vsevolod Meyerhold: Maeterlinck's *Sister Beatrice* and Blok's *The Puppet Booth*. Tairov grew discontent with Meyerhold's dictatorial nature, believing the actor, under Meyerhold, was reduced to a purely decorative or picturesque role and was denied any creative input into the production.

Tairov left the Komissarzhevskaya company to join the Mobile Theatre, first as an actor and later as director. It was with this touring company that Tairov became acquainted with the theatre of realism. Just as he became disillusioned with the restrictive practices of Meyerhold's stylized theatre, Tairov eventually came to dislike the naturalistic theatre for the same reasons.

Rather than placing the actor under a dictatorial director, the naturalistic theatre made the actor subservient to the literal representation of a playscript and "to truth to life with all its fortuitous circumstance...."[1] The objective of the naturalistic theatre was to produce on stage a photographic portrayal of reality; Naturalism suffered from "a dysentery of formlessness," from a lack of aesthetic design and aesthetic forms.[2]

Tairov sought a "synthetic theatre" that combined the devices of ballet, opera, circus, and variety show with the "legitimate" theatre. In the mise-en-scène, he intended to organically fuse the scenic elements into a dynamic synthesis, "a synthesis of emotion and form,"[3] using the unrestricted creative and physical faculties of the actor as the keystone to the production.

Tairov referred to his theatre as "the theatre of neo-realism" because it was created by the "real art of the actor and, within the limits of theatrical truth, real scenic atmosphere."[4] Neo-realism was not an attempt to copy nature but to create an artistically conceived scenic reality in which the incongruity between the static two-dimensional scenery and the dynamic three-dimensional actor was eliminated. Tairov believed that the body was the actor's *material* and that it was best displayed only in three-dimensional environs. Tairov sought to redesign the stage around the actor. The stage could be "worked out only in a definite cubic capacity"[5] if it was to harmonize with the human body.

At the Moscow Kamerny Theatre, which he founded in 1914, Tairov hoped to construct a stage that would accommodate the actor. The scene designer was discouraged from painting picturesque panels and backdrops; his task was to restore to the theatre the significance of the stage floor; the playing area needed to be divided into various horizontal and raked platforms and surfaces, all of different heights. Only in this way could the gestures, movements, and formations of the actors be effectively presented and the material of the actor put to its greatest use. The planes and levels would not only give the spectator a better view of the actors on stage, of "the whole corps-de-théâtre"[6], but also give to the actor numerous possibilities for vertical, as well as horizontal, movement and plastic gesture and form.

The horizontal and vertical surfaces produced a series of three-dimensional forms and structures; these were intended "solely to provide that indispensable rhythm and plastic base for the actor's display of his art...."[7] Tairov pared the stage to essential props and his actors' gestures to highly expressive succinct forms and organized all scenic elements into a synthesis of what he believed to be the underlying rhythm of the play. The end of this rhythmic synthesis was to integrate the actor and setting to such a degree that the design of the scene seemed to originate in the rhythmic and plastic aspects of the actors. Abraham Efros noted that Tairov replaced "the old-fashioned academical poses and gestures; a classicism of pure form replaced a classicism of historical imitation" and created "a broad rhythm in their [the actors'] gestures...."[8]

Tairov arranged his productions so that their rhythmic flow resembled what he believed to be the purest art: music. Design, sound, lighting, movement, and speech were, in a sense, "composed" on a musical basis and were intended to be visual equivalents of melodies and harmonies. Tairov described the way in which stairs and platforms produced a musical impression in the spectator:

> This...depends entirely on your rhythmic intent. If you wish the spectator to receive the impression that the Virgin descends almost without touching the earth; if you wish to attach a solemn, liturgical character to the action of the descent, you will construct the steps so that the intervals between them are everywhere the same. They correspond rhythmically to 1/4 or 1/8 time, in this way giving to the movement of the actress an even and uninterrupted, flowing rhythm.[9]

Music was, for Tairov, the only means by which a director could achieve emotional form and scenic synthesis. He insisted that lighting and costume should be "orchestrated" into a rhythmic and plastic correspondence with the other scenic elements and that the entire assortment of scenic devices should accentuate the art of the actor, showing his material in imaginative and precise scenic effects. Design was not in the service of verisimilitude but of artistic or creative musical intents.

Norris Houghton writes in *Moscow Rehearsals* that by discarding naturalistic devices and embracing instead an innovative, "pure formalistic style," Tairov welcomed to his theatre the formal features of Cubism and Futurism, as well as "a Constructivism based on form and not on function."[10] Fuerst and Hume remark that if Cubism was to claim some jurisdiction in the theatre, it was to sit comfortably in Tairov's productions at The Kamerny Theatre.[11] Tairov composed several productions in a Cubistic manner, giving a plastic and synthetical treatment to, among others, *Famira Kifared, L'Annonce Faite à Marie,* and *Phaedre.*

Famira Kifared (1916)

Tairov staged Annenski's tragedy, *Famira Kifared,* at the Moscow Kamerny Theatre in 1916. His concern in this production was with rhythmic movement created through the interaction of actor, stage, and decor. He commissioned Alexandra Exter, a Russian avant-garde artist, to execute the sets and costumes and to research the dynamic possibilities of the stage floor.

Exter was, beside Lyubov Popova and Varvara Stepanova, one of the few avant-garde artists to work in the theatre on a regular basis. John Bowlt writes in his preface to the catalogue for the exhibition, "Stage Design and the Russian Avant-Garde," that Exter was successful in transcending "the confines of the pictorial surface" to manage three-dimensional stage space because she was particularly adept at organizing "forms in their interaction with space."[12]

It was largely through Exter's work that the stage space for productions such as *Famira Kifared* became "a dynamic mechanism."[13] Bowlt quotes the Russian critic, Yakov Tugendkhold, who observed that Exter and Tairov achieved "an organic connection between the moving actors and the objects at rest" and had, in the process, resorted to "the dynamic *use of immobile forms.*"[14]

Basing his production plan for *Famira Kifared* on rhythmic patterns and action, Tairov decided to exploit the three-dimensional features of the floor of the stage so that his actors had the greatest opportunities for movement through space and for achieving the two principal rhythmic patterns of the production: "The bacchanalian and satyrical rhythms of Dionysos, and the smooth-flowing regular sensation of Apollonian rhythms."[15]

Exter expressed the Apollonian rhythm in a series of broad, escalating platforms that were piled to create a solid staircase across the center upstage area. The open area behind the platforms continued the smooth and tranquil escalating rhythm of the stairs and, at the same time, provided a strong contrast to the conglomeration of conical forms at the sides of the stage. The tall cones, squat cubes and blocks, all assembled in an irregular order and pulsating rhythm, were visual representations of "the multi-formity of rhythmic variation characteristic of the Cult of Dionysos."[16] Through the contrast of rhythms and forms, Exter expressed the conflict between the cults of Apollo and Dionysos.

Exter's set for *Famira Kifared* has been referred to as a Cubist design. Efros wrote: "It was as though Cubism were on parade. . ." and referred to the dominating "harmony of masses."[17] Narrow staircases to the sides, the center platforms and simple movable geometric forms placed over the set broke the stage into sharp angles and levels. In addition, tall cones, upright rectangular boxes, and flattened columns ascended the sides of the set and gave the stage picture a strong, vertical, and voluminous appearance; these objects contributed to what Efros called a "cubic academism" or "cubic baroque."[18] Bowlt has described the several designs by Exter as "lyrical adaptations of Cubism and Constructivism."[19]

In all this "cubic academism" and "lyrical adaptations of Cubism," Exter actually produced a stage set that resembled to a great extent the paintings of Synthetic Cubism. Although the scene was depicted in an assemblage of familial, architectonic forms—the forms being geometric abstractions of the stone pillars and columns of classical temples—Exter's intention was not so much to produce the shallow landscape that characterized Analytic Cubism as it was to accentuate the plasticity, the sculptural presence, of Synthetic Cubism.

As the Cubists dissociated the subject from its normal appearance in order to produce a plastic effect by integrating the object and its environs, Exter portrayed the classical architecture in the sharp angles and levels of the set pieces; rather than blend all the scenic elements into one diffuse landscape, she retained the hard edges and contours of the forms, making them appear sculpted and thrusted. Exter accentuated the three-dimensional qualities of each form; she sculpted plastic icons in keeping with Tairov's demand that stage surfaces were to provide a plastic base for the actor.

Tairov, like Meyerhold, "choreographed" his actors into independent perceptual areas. Set against the low background of sculpted architectonic forms were groups or concentrations of actors that divided the stage picture into a number of visual areas, each with its own nucleus. The actors in one scene, for example, essentially composed two autonomous perceptual groups on the stage picture surface: a group of ten actors on the left and a group of two on the right.

The ten actors on the left formed a dense, voluminous, elliptical sphere around the satyr with the string instrument. The irregular ellipse consisted of five actors looking upward into the flies, two sitting on the right and looking upward toward stage left and two sitting in front, facing each other with a gap between them; standing in the center of this opening was the satyr, the nucleus of the elliptical gestalt. Tairov arranged each of the actors on the periphery so that they were visually connected by pose and psychologism. It seemed that each actor appreciated the satyr's music.

The visual area of two actors at the right gained its autonomy through its distance from the larger, denser area on the left. The nucleus here lay in the male figure and was reinforced by the female figure who looked downward at him. This area was connected to the other by the woman's lean toward the left and the man's glance in the same direction.

What Tairov created in this scene was, in effect, two independent visual gestalts of contrasting density and volume within the geometric abstraction of the background. Each had a specific character and was self-sufficient. Yet the two gestalts also seemed to belong together, visually connected by the male and female figures in the stage-left group. Tairov, like Meyerhold, ordered his actors into autonomous gestalts that were subservient to or integrated with the overall stage picture. It was through the associations of the individual parts of each group and of attitudes and qualities common to all groups that a pictorial logic emerged. The pictorial gestalts were formalistically related to the generic geometric shapes and voluminous densities in the background.

There was, however, in this production a weaker, less direct, perceptual, formal connection to the shapes in the architecture of the background. The postures and poses of Tairov's actors were not exact repetitions of the severe and angular lines of the levels, cones, and cubes. Somewhat rounded and hypertrophied, almost organically conceived, the physical pose appeared ornamental and "soft" against the bold set construction.

Where Meyerhold used the background as a *visual model* for choreographing his actors in *The Magnificent Cuckold,* Tairov played down the visual interconnectedness between actor and set in *Famira Kifared*, preferring to use the background as a *rhythmical model* for organizing gesture and pose. Both directors sought to integrate the plastic aspects of the set, but Tairov was more interested in a rhythmic synthesis than a one-to-one visual correspondence; for this reason, the formal dialogue between foreground and background, which was so obvious in Meyerhold's *Cuckold,* was less directly expressed in Tairov's *Famira Kifared.*

Given Tairov's preoccupation with the rhythmic synthesis of actor and set and the cubified nature of Exter's design, the movement of Tairov's actors over the stage should have had obvious similarities to the sensation of movement in Cubist paintings. The Cubists produced a sensation of movement by exaggerating the staccato rhythm in the interaction of forms and by integrating foreground and background elements in plastic transfiguration; a dynamism of forms, a rhythmic interaction of shapes emerged. The abrupt divisions between shapes and masses interacting in pictorial space produced an abrupt and staggered rhythm across the picture plane. Tairov arranged groups of actors in visual gestalts over the stage, creating volumes and masses on the Cubistic landscape. The volumes and masses of actors were arranged and ordered like the planes and shapes in Synthetic Cubism: overlapping dense areas arranged in an ascending order, the distance between them being an echo of the distance between sculpted forms in the background. Although Tairov was less interested in a strong formal interconnectedness between actor and set, he did reproduce the sensation of movement found in Synthetic Cubism by juxtaposing the flattened, geometric surfaces (on the set) and contrasting volumes (in the groups of actors).

In one instance, for example, Tairov placed two groups, or volumes, of actors at each side of a standing, central figure. The three areas took on a sculptural presence and receded vertically in space against the flat, dense, and escalating architectonic forms in Exter's set. These three gestalts, or volumes, were defined first by their distance from each other in space and by their weight or density in contrast to the dull and low rectangular forms of the central stairway and the blank open background; like the volumes of dark conical shapes to either side of the central stairway, the masses of actors were juxtaposed, thrusted volumes on the landscape.

If Tairov's theory of rhythmic synthesis was practically viable and if the actors moved in accord with the lines of the side, staircases, and geometric forms, then any movement in or by these volumes would have been abrupt and, perhaps, angular. A staccato rhythm would have emerged from the sequence of juxtaposed flat surfaces and contrasting, sculpted volumes.

Huntley Carter concludes that the levels, volumes, and geometric forms in Exter's set "offered the best solution to the stage and scenic problem of rhythmic synthesis."[20] His conclusion is founded on the belief that the multi-leveled, vertical construction of geometric design and proportion forced on the actor a corresponding geometric movement. "The actor," he writes, "by jumping from one level to another, set up different oscillations and different wave lengths of movement."[21]

Tairov's description of the "dynamic impression of the bacchanal" corroborates Carter's belief. Tairov explains in *Notes of a Director* the manner in which he achieved the dynamism of the bacchanalian scenes:

In accord with the changed rhythmic goal, you would break up the stage so that the levels of various heights would be connected by various and multiformed rhythms. Thanks to these the bacchanalian movement and satyrical leaps, acquiring the varied and multiformed undulations peculiar to the whole structure, would create the requisite dynamic impression of the bacchanal.[22]

Given the cubified design of the set piece, the "different oscillations and different wave lengths of movement," and the "multiformed undulations peculiar to the whole structure," it could be assumed that the actors' movements over the set resembled the undulating and varietal rhythm of forms in Cubist paintings. The abrupt movement and gestures of Tairov's actors, like the rapid succession of small disjointed images in Cubism, created a staccato, stroboscopic impression. By contrast, the smooth, central apollonia sections would necessitate a smooth, flowing movement.

Famira Kifared was perhaps the first of Tairov's productions to reflect a Cubist aesthetic and was by no means the most thorough or successful of these experiments. In Racine's *Salome* (1917), Tairov continued to research the practicable viability of multiformed levels, Cubistic architectonic background, and the dynamic transformation and synthesis of the mise-en-scène. It was not until 1920, with the production of Paul Claudel's *L'Annonce Faite à Marie,* that Tairov achieved a stage picture that bore a close visual resemblance to Cubist paintings.

L'Annonce Faite à Marie (1920)

Tairov invited Alexander Vesnin, an architect, to design the set and costumes for the production of *L'Annonce Faite à Marie* by Paul Claudel. Vesnin brought to his designs the bold, massive, and severe appearance of primordial architecture, copying "the gothicism of the cathedrals, reduced to its primal elements."[23] In the foreword to the photographic history of Tairov's productions, *The Artists of the Kamerni Theatre,* Efros writes that this production was Vesnin's "first Cubist composition in the theatre" and that the basis of his interpretation was "a Cubist gothicism."[24]

Where Vesnin's Cubistic set differed from Exter's Cubist-influenced designs for *Famira Kifared* was in his use of an Analytic technique. Photographs of the set reveal a close correspondence with the flattened landscapes of large, heavily contoured blocks in the early Cubist paintings. It seems that Vesnin's interest was to build a tightly integrated, shallow, and escalating field of dispersed geometric shapes rather than arrange independent planes, masses, or volumes in a highly sculpted pictorial field.

The stage picture consisted primarily of massive geometric forms and exhibited a closed planar structure similar to that in Picasso's *Houses on a Hill.* Heavy trapezoids, rectangles, voluminous columns, vertical stairs, and large flat planes acted as shelves, platforms, and backgrounds for the actors and statuary. Each unit was solid and was well-defined by its weight and its strong, hard-edged contours. The set pieces resembled the closed architectural shapes in Analytic Cubism; massive frontal planes and volumes laid on top of and in front of one another, seeming to compete for space. The many disparate, abstract objects were fused by their mass and shape into one architectonic surface.

Vesnin distorted the subject, an interior of a cathedral to describe its formal presence. He altered the primal anatomical features of the subject to accentuate its abstract, architectural construction.

Two large pieces of religious statuary were placed against the Cubistic background at either side of the stage. A candelabra of thick white cylindrical tubes sat on an octagonal pedestal just right of stage center to the rear. These three properties were architectonic distortions of real objects but bore a close enough resemblance to denote a cathedral chamber. As in Analytic Cubism, the bold architectonic design and accentuated contours of the objects made them intelligible, although each shape participated in a landscape of familial shapes.

Vesnin based his costumes on a similar, if not identical, pattern. The rendering for Marie's gown showed a strong Cubist influence in that the lines of the smock and skirt beneath divided and faceted the anatomy into a series of bold geometric solids. The skirt made the legs appear as one striated column. The smock also flattened the chest into a broad plane with crisscrossing lines that divided the torso in irregular geometric patterns; the sleeves of the smock terminated just above the elbow in boldly marked "V" shapes and covered a blouse with full sleeves pulled tight at the cuff; the arm, consequently, assumed a voluminous appearance. The head was covered by what appeared to be a stiff, cloth circle, with the face of the character placed in the center of the circular head piece.

The actual costume for this character was a faithful copy of the rendering. The only significant difference between the two was that the lines dividing the torso in the actual costume quartered the anatomy rather than faceting it into a pattern of irregular geometric shapes.

Other costumes reflected Vesnin's interest in geometricizing the human anatomy. Flat chest shields and "A" line skirts sectioned the body into a square and trapezoid; thick white leggings under loose-topped dark boots made cylinders of the feet and legs; a heavy, folded cape appeared as a dense planar backdrop to full sleeves, and a cylindrical cap with an elliptical brim flattened the head.

Other costumes draped the entire body in cloth, the folds concealing the body and cutting it into longitudinal columns. Three-quarter length smocks with geometric patterns divided the bodies into halves, the geometric design giving the actor an architectural presence. Head gear generally concealed the skeletal features of the head and face and reshaped the skull in conical, spherical, or planar abstraction.

Rendering both set construction and costumes in closed, essential geometric shapes, Vesnin gave the stage picture a surface/depth dialogue of forms similar to that in Analytic Cubism. Placed against the Cubistic patterns in the set piece and draped in costumes that reflected the Cubistic shapes behind them, the actors on stage resembled the dispersed fragments of geometric forms on a Cubist painting. The dark and light tones created by the folds in the cloth and the bold planar and geometric patterns were microscopic repetitions of the set design. The pleats in Marie's skirt not only resembled the folds in the stage curtains but also suggested the design of the voluminous octagonal pedestal. The rectilinear torso, the cylindrical legs and hat of the soldier looked like fragments chiseled from the background or from other garments. The dark and light contrasts in the Cubistic patterns on the costumes precisely echoed the contrasts in the planar architecture of the surrounding walls and props.

Tairov and Vesnin produced an architectural unity in the stage picture in the same way that the Cubist painters fused object and field: abandoning illusionism for geometric abstraction, each sought to accentuate the structural interaction of field and object so that the essential features of the subjects were no longer only "seen" but became the basis of "seen forms."

Efros finds the structural and stylistic synthesis of set, props, and costumes to be an interesting notion but actually detrimental to the rhythmic and histrionic tasks of the actors. He complains that the "Cubo-Gothic costumes were as coffins" which "did not assist the actor so much as determine his carriage and gestures. His movements...seemed to melt in this architecture of costume."[25] It can be deduced from Efros' remarks that the actors in this production were either forced by their costumes or instructed by Tairov to gesticulate and pose in an angular, perhaps mechanized fashion. Both of these possibilities may have been true since Tairov has written that costume "is a new means for enriching the expressiveness of the actor's gesture, for with the help of a genuine costume every acting gesture should acquire special clarity...depending on its artistic intent."[26]

The photographs of *L'Annonce Faite à Marie* show that if Tairov instructed his actors in a "Cubistic" movement, several actors failed to carry out his instructions successfully. There does not appear to be a serious or uniform attempt on the part of the actors to repeat in their gestures the rectilinear and architectonic design in the background. For example, while a soldier in one scene struck an angular, rigid pose, bending stiffly at the knees and waist, Marie's pose, by contrast, was less severe, less stylized. The same discrepancy in gesture and pose occurs in group scenes where some actors appear more rigid and angular than others.

The lack of uniformity in gesture and pose corroborates Efros' contention that the costumes were actually a hindrance to the actors. It appears that whatever angular, rectilinear, or geometric gestures occurred in the production were probably imposed on the actors by the bulky and cumbersome "Cubo-Gothic costumes."

What makes Efros' observations even more plausible are the photos from Tairov's production of *Phaedre*, in which every actor on stage seems to reproduce in gesture and pose the Cubistic lines in the background. *Phaedre* was perhaps the one production in which Tairov most successfully and completely utilized a Cubistic aesthetics to create a thorough integration and synthesis in the "scenic atmosphere."

Phaedre (1922)

Compared to *Famira Kifared* and *L'Annonce Faite à Marie,* Tairov's production of *Phaedre* demonstrated a more sophisticated and refined application of the Cubist sensibility. Basic geometric forms, the "primordial crystals"[27] of Tairov's scenic art, decorated the stage but were subtlely and sparsely applied; the rudimentary integration of cubic space and cubic gestures in the earlier productions matured into a formalistic synthesis of Cubistic figures, properties, and movement. Tairov produced a flattened stage picture in which the lines, angles, and proportions of the scenery and the bodies of the actors were successfully blended into a plastically conceived, homogenous landscape of familial forms, planes, and volumes. It was as though Tairov had resolved the problems he encountered in giving Cubistic treatments to previous productions. Fuerst and Hume attribute Tairov's accomplishment to the "appropriateness of Cubism [where] a concern for plasticity arises in the mise-en-scène."[28]

Tairov commissioned Alexander Vesnin to design the set and costumes for the production of Racine's mythological tragedy. As with *L'Annonce Faite à Marie,* Vesnin resorted to an architectural basis for his designs, liberally translating the massive geometric forms of ancient Greek architecture in a modern, Cubistic fashion. Vesnin splintered the stage space in Cubist style, reducing the set to an abstract assemblage of enormous centrifugal cones, triangles, cylinders, and sloping planes. The dominant forms on stage were the tall, voluminous cylinders at either side that had been mounted on top of broad platforms and built into the flies. Other cylindrical and spherical objects had been placed over the stage; on the right, Vesnin constructed several parallelograms and divided the stage floor into two stairways, or staggered sloping platforms, that eventually met downstage center.

Gorchakov refers to a "limitless blue background,"[29] but Vesnin's sketches of the set and photographs of the production exhibit several triangular panels mounted between the solid, heavy back wall and the columns. In addition, Vesnin suspended colored geometric hangings and strands of rope from above; these articles cut across the background and divided it into geometric shapes that appeared as abstract architectonic forms dispersed through a two-dimensional space.

Vesnin and Tairov interpreted the archaic and primordial spirit of Greek mythology as a geometrical landscape: "the stairs resembled crags on a cliff, and the columns looked like the portal to a temple,"[30] ". . . colored hangings, which, crossed by ropes, gave the illusion of sails, hawsers and prow of a Greek ship";[31] "the cylinder at the right gave an interpretation of the classical column" while the parallelograms "contributed an archaic quality to the entire scheme."[32] Vesnin's method of schematizing the stage space repeated the method by which Cubist artists composed their paintings. The formal presence of the scene was distorted, reduced to underlying essential geometric shapes, and then rearranged in a flattened, architectonic construction of intersecting and overlapping planes and volumes. So exact was Vesnin's Cubistic motif that it inspired Efros to write: "This was in reality a Cubist neo-classicism."[33]

Vesnin designed the costumes on the same principle: "Cubist neo-classicism." His sketch of Phaedre's costume resembled the sketches he made for *L'Annonce Faite à Marie:* enormous, multi-folded overgarments gave the torso a striated, voluminous appearance; a skirt or tunic beneath made a cylinder of the lower anatomy, and decorous capes and shawls fragmented the body into a pattern of geometric forms. The actual costume was a faithful reconstruction of the Cubist-influenced design of the original drawing; with the addition of a many-faceted, broad plated cap and semicircular, stiff plummage, the costume imparted an architectonic construction to the human anatomy.

Other costumes for this production imparted the same appearance. An Hellenic tunic, for example, reflected the architectural pattern in the set. The short skirt consisted of many rectilinear pieces of fabric, draped over one another in the way that the large hangings draped the architectonic forms on stage. The top of the tunic bisected the chest into two triangles joined at their bases and distinguished from each other by contrasting tones. The cylindrical shape of the legs was accentuated by tightly wrapped buskins and elevated shoes, and the arms were covered by cylindrical arm-plates that disappeared at the elbow into the full short sleeves. In addition, Vesnin conceived head-gear and hand props, such as swords, shields, and spears, in austere geometric forms. The Hellenic garb and small props repeated the geometric shapes contained in the set piece; placed in and around the Cubistic forms that made up the set, the cubified actor entered a formalistic interaction with the objects on stage.

Designing set and costumes in a Cubistic style, Vesnin and Tairov created a highly integrated, homogenous picture surface in which the scenic figure and set were fused in an architectonic unity. The stage picture essentially formed a vertical, planar grid ruptured at points by the geometric shapes of the hangings and actors' costumes. The human figure and stage pieces, like the assortment of geometric forms in Picasso's *Ma Jolie, originated in and precipitated* pictorial space and participated equally as structural elements in the continuum of the picture surface. In this way, the stage space contained the actor, and the actor the space, so that actor and space were united in one homogenous pictorial landscape. There was in Tairov's mise-en-scène some visual resemblance to the surface/depth dialogue that distinguished Cubist paintings.

While costumes and background seemed to blend with one another into a shallow, tilted landscape, the raked and multi-leveled floor prevented the stage picture from becoming totally flat; the stage floor contributed a three-dimensional quality to the stage picture through its descending, forward thrust. The set did not swallow, or envelope, the actor but functioned in the same cubic space as a tilted or inclined *base* for his movements. This feature was, of course, a principal tenet in Tairov's theatre: the three-dimensional surfaces on the stage should provide a plastic base for the actor.

Tairov joined the physical cubic capacities of actor and space by preserving a sensation of depth in the flattened stage picture surface; in actuality, he repeated the process by which the Cubist painters preserved a plastic, sculptural presence. The stage forms, despite their formalistic affinity with the background, pressed outward toward the auditorium whenever placed on the raked ramps and platforms.

Tairov also increased the sculptural and plastic impression of his actors through color contrast. Gorchakov reports that three warriors dressed in brown garb "were as static and ponderous as the columns against the limitless blue background"; yet he adds that the "shining indigo background set off the characters and transformed them into statues."[34]

Elevating the actors on sloping platforms, accentuating their plasticity through color contrast, Tairov put a distance between the scenic figure and the background masses and curtailed the surface/depth dialogue of cubified forms and shapes in the stage picture. His stage forms, like the pictorial forms in Synthetic Cubism, assumed a sculptural, plastic presence.

The plastic and sculpted qualities of the costumed bodies and properties on stage were transferred through Tairov's direction to gesture and pose; the acting in *Phaedre* was orchestrated to conform or harmonize with the Cubist forms of the set. In Tairov's Kamerny Theatre, scenic surfaces and platforms not only provided a plastic base for the actors but also functioned as a model for their gestures and postures and determined, to a great extent, the rhythm of the actors' movements. Tairov enhanced the histrionic rhythms of his actors by formalizing movement into what Norris Houghton calls "aesthetic abstractions."[35] Judging from the photographs of actors in *Phaedre*, these "aesthetic abstractions" of movement reflected or repeated the austere, angular, and rectilinear patterns of the Cubist set and costumes.

The geometrical features of pose and gesture were particularly noticeable in group scenes. In one of these scenes, a soldier stood downstage left, at the bottom of the spiraling stairway. The soldier stood frontally, the patchwork skirt and broad breastplates of the tunic giving the figure a flattened, geometric appearance. The soldier's body leaned sharply to the left, following the left-handed descent of the stairway. The left foot was planted on the surface below the right foot, and the left arm, which was placed on the flat top of a cube, supported the leaning figure. The left leg was wrapped with a shin guard, giving that part of the leg a cylindrical shape, and was bent in a severe angle at the knee. The actor's body resembled a flat, Cubistic plane composed of geometric forms; it not only repeated shapes contained in the set, but, in leaning stage left, it echoed and continued the descending momentum of the stairway. It would not be difficult to imagine the staccato, perhaps machine-like motions that character would make when moving.

The same could be said of another figure on the far right of the stage. His cloak looked like a solid and broad rectilinear plane, his extended arms and spread legs demarcating the extremities. The other two figures on stage also reflected the forms and rhythms in the set. The statuesque, upright, linear pose of the woman reflected the cylindrical shape and vertical thrust of the columns behind her; the contrasts of light and dark tones in her costume resembled the contrasts in the background and accentuated her formal similarity to the design of the set. The rigidity of her pose suggested a plastic, statuesque quality in her movements.

The character in front of the woman leaned backwards, following the ascending momentum of the stairway. He, too, was placed frontally, the broad shape of his cloak giving his figure a planar appearance, the light and dark contrasts of his costume an echo of the background. The left arm was held out parallel to the platform, his left leg straight, making a diagonal vector that seemed to intersect with the diagonal curb behind him. This pose appears to be similar to that of the soldier, only tilted in the opposite direction. It also would not be difficult to imagine that this character might move like the soldier, in stiff, large, staccato gestures. Alexander Efros notes that the actors in this production, as if guided by the plasticity of the forms in the Cubistic set and costumes, exhibited "a broad rhythm in the gestures...."[36]

Other scenes in *Phaedre* displayed similar postures and gestures and indicated the "broad rhythm" and angular movements of Tairov's actors. Tairov directed one actor to kneel on one knee and bend his body forward and slightly upward along the line of the platform. The actor's weight was supported by the left leg, which rested flat against the floor and was bent at the knee. His back was only slightly arched, enough to permit the head to fall downward in a sharp angle at the neck. The left fist was clenched and the cylindrical arm bent at the elbow following the flow of the back and head. The right arm was bent in a similar manner and was propped on the right knee. Together, the rigidly angled arms formed a triangular plane across the torso. The right leg bent upwards, also in a rigid and severe angle.

This pose, an "aesthetic abstraction," reproduced the architectonic forms and lines of the set. The left shin formed a parallel line to the diagonal, raised rail and the base of the triangle behind the actor; the left thigh and arm created virtual lines that repeated the flow of the rope to the actor's right; the triangular plane across the torso repeated the triangular wedge in the background; the right shin and arm paralleled the hanging strand of rope, and the right thigh created a diagonal with the rear rail. Not only was this figure arranged in abstraction but in *geometric, architectural abstraction.*

If the set provided an "indispensable rhythm" for the movements of the actor, and the actor was, as has been pointed out, sculpted along the plastic lines of the Cubistic set, then the actor probably moved and gesticulated in geometric, *Cubistic abstraction.* This would have been the most likely manner of motion, given Tairov's concern with the total integration of actor and set, with a rhythmic synthesis.

It can be assumed, then, that the movement of Tairov's actors, who were depicted in Cubistic abstraction, resembled the sensation of movement created by Cubistic forms on canvas: a staccato, rhythmic synthesis of architectonic forms, a rhythmic interaction of shapes rendered in plastic transfiguration. Gorchakov implies this much when he writes:

> The costumes, the poses, and the motions and gestures. Everything trifling and superficial was removed.... There were severe statues in stone, animated only by niggardly motions and gestures....[37]

It was through the formalistic exchange of plastic icons in the background and foreground and through rhythmic synthesis that Tairov achieved in the mise-en-scène what Gleizes and Metzinger referred to as "the integration of the plastic consciousness." In effect, the actor functioned in the cubic space of his surroundings; the spatial characteristics of the set defined for him the shape and tone of his movement and posture. In this way, the actor and set became equal paradigmatic components in the pictorial space, the objects and shapes in the environs becoming, like the mobile actors, *events* in the perceptual field of the stage.

As equal paradigmatic events, the set pieces, props, and actors were not only integrated by their formal identities and spatial interaction but also in time. The spectator did not perceive an actor set against a background nor the actor separated in time from the set. The spectator perceived the actor and set in a continuum that was formalistically defined as a surface/depth dialogue. The actor and set were perceived at the same moment in the same field. Space and time, then, participated in one functional relationship, a four-dimensional space-time continuum.

When Mordecai Gorelik observed that the "actor's movements became defined for him by the spatial arrangement of the setting,"[38] he neglected to add that the actor had, through his form and movement, a reciprocal function. The pictorial space, the mise-en-scène, for Tairov's *Phaedre* resembled the pictorial space in Cubist paintings in that it was not a mere container for events but a part of the continuum of the events within it.

6

Fernand Léger and the
Theatre of Spectacle

Fernand Léger and the Theatre of Spectacle

Fernand Léger invented his own brand of Cubism. It was a style that simultaneously embraced the innovations of Picasso and Braque, and yet it included certain distinctive devices that made Léger's paintings unique within the circle of Cubist painters. Léger mentioned in 1931 that he had always been on the periphery of the Cubist fraternity. "Personally," he wrote, "I have stayed at the 'edge' without ever involving myself totally in their radical concept, which is the last word in tendentious research."[1] While Léger painted flattened, formally integrated, and homogenous landscapes of geometric shapes, he added a sensation of dynamism in the contrast of static forms and, after the example of his close friend Robert Delaunay, vibrant colors and hard-edged imagery.

Léger's decisive break with the mainstream of Cubist painters came in 1918 when he returned to Paris after serving with the French artillery in the First World War. During his tour of duty, Léger encountered the heavy artillery machinery and became fascinated with their design. He recalled being "dazzled by the breach of a seventy-five millimeter gun which was standing uncovered in the sunlight: the magic of light on white metal."[2] The aesthetic and formal devices of Analytic Cubism ceased to be effective expressive vehicles, and Léger turned to the sketches he made of military machinery; propellers, cam shafts, ball bearings, fusilages, cannon barrels, and other hard metal instruments began to appear in his paintings. These Léger painted in the flattened, geometric patterns typical of other Cubist works, but he accentuated the metallic aspect of the machines, a preference that has prompted historians to refer to this period as the *mechanical phase*.[3]

Léger was inspired during his mechanical period by manufactured goods, commercial posters, and urbanscapes. Henning Rischbieter writes in *Art and the Stage in the 20th Century* that, of the great modern painters,

Léger was the one who turned most decisively and with most enthusiastic approval to the big city, technology, and the poster. He considered his painting "realistic" because it was composed of objects from the man-made world.[4]

And Max Kozloff comments in *Cubism/Futurism:*

For him [Léger], the city is a vernacular uninhabited *now*, a frozen industrial landscape in vital bad taste. It is composed of still lifes scanned and concentrated in an imaginary jump-cut space (resembling the long shots and close-ups of the movies) and materialized, finally in the guise of advertising and road signs.[5]

Léger's obsession with modernity and a machine aesthetic was evidenced in his paintings between 1918 and 1924. He created in these six years a series of highly abstract paintings, the first important post-war canvases being *La Partie de Cartes* and *The City*. These paintings revealed Léger's attempt to reconcile his interest in industrial goods and the devices of Analytic Cubism; he soon discovered "the loose and impressionistic style of his pre-war Cubist canvases incapable of rendering this new subject matter."[6] Léger consequently developed a style of painting in which the primary concern was not with abstraction but with the physical presence of the *object*. He took for his subject "the spirit of the times"[7] and the manufactured objects that manifested its meaning.

Léger declared, "I look only at the object"[8] and began to render strong, close-up, and graphic portrayals of objects in the industrial and commercial landscape. The object provided Léger with raw material for his paintings, and he responded first to its plastic and sculptural values, believing that the modern object was independent of the interpretative and descriptive value generally given to it by its function. The modern object had, in its plastic beauty, an interior value that was "strictly absolute, independent of what it represents."[9]

Contemporary life could be explained as the revolt of the "personality of the objects"[10] against humanity, and it was man's responsibility to direct objects to their equal, if not superior, station. Objects asserted their autonomy through movement and proliferation; lights, colors, manikins, billboards, buildings, all objects became mobile, living entities and commanded attention. The object in modern society represented a pivotal event between the past and the future; modern art was to glorify, if not deify, the object.

Léger believed that commerce and industry first interpreted objects "in a manner suited to the stage," manifesting their plastic and scenic values in order to attract and entrance the consumer:

The efforts made by commerce have reached such a height that a mannequin display put on by a couturier of quality equals and even surpasses, in its spectacle value, many medieval stage scenes.[11]

Artists were to follow the example of commerce and to scour the environment for objects with theatrical potential; the idea of creativity in the modern age was to manifest the "enormous spectacle value"[12] of common and everyday objects.

In essence, Léger suggested that modern commodities, in their plastic and scenic qualities, were not only suitable raw materials for artists but that they could also be employed as scenic forms in a new concept of theatrical activity: *a theatre of spectacle*. Léger's notion of a theatre of spectacle evolved not only from his obsession with a modern spirit and its by-products but also from several problems he found in conventional theatre; the solutions to these problems lay in the nature of the object.

Léger looked on the auditorium as a dull and dark mausoleum for indifferent and inattentive audiences. The real problem with the auditorium lay in the fact that the footlights, "a neutral, dangerous space,"[13] made it difficult for the performer to reach and engage the spectator. If the theatre was to be at all effective, it must somehow cross the footlights "in order to go and ensnare the gentleman who came to get away from it all."[14]

Léger proposed not to eliminate the division between stage and auditorium but actually to enhance it by underlining what he thought to be at the heart of effective theatre: the inverse proportion between the presentation and the audience. To cross the footlights and engage the spectator,

there must be a maximum of stage effects; the axiom that "the state of the stage must be inversely proportional to the state of the auditorium" must be proved.[15]

Léger reasoned that the nature of the auditorium was determined by darkness, passivity, and quiet, whereas the stage, when properly outfitted, became a dynamic sector of light, color, rapid activity, and noise. The theatrical presentation must be a total invention, an inverse of the nature of reality.

What was particularly interesting about this notion of an effective theatre was that, while Léger advocated an inverse proportion between stage and auditorium, between presentation and reality, it was in reality, in daily occurrences that Léger found the model for his Theatre of Spectacle. "To talk about spectacle," he wrote in 1924, "is to imagine the world in all its daily visual manifestations."[16] Léger looked to the streets, the boulevards, and the highways for sources of entertainment; he discovered in these commonplace arenas spectacles offering greater pleasure and value than the ballet or drama: "On the boulevards two men are transporting enormous gilded letters on a barrow. The effect is so unexpected that everyone stops to look."[17]

Léger placed the origin of the modern spectacle in these everyday scenes and advised theatre artists to entertain their audiences in the same way that shopkeepers and the Church entertained pedestrians and congregations.

The Catholic religion has also known how to make use of these methods to steer men according to its instruction....it has pushed the art of the spectacle very far.... The Church understood long ago that man is drawn instinctively to the brillant, luminous colored object. It adopted music and song. If it has imposed itself on the world, that is because it has not neglected any of the visual and auditory means of its epoch.[18]

The Theatre of Spectacle was a theatre of invention, and its value derived from the ability of its objects to entrance the audience with their luminous and dynamic, mundane features. The Theatre of Spectacle found delight and surprise in the most commonplace scenes.

The modern world was, for Léger, a world of speed. The high velocity of the urban age compressed events and objects into a rapid series of hypertrophied visual images; these images would collide with one another, briefly assert themselves, then be pushed on by the momentum of the urban and machine spirit. Although the rapidity of the passing scenes produced a series of enlarged and contrasting images, it was also the tie that bound and united the individual scenes, creating an order and a unified spectacle from the contrasting episodes.

If the Theatre of Spectacle was successfully to convey the spirit of modernity, it was to present and unify its objects, images, and scenes in speed. Léger was quite specific about the velocity with which each spectacle in a panorama of scenes should pass. He warned that the spectacle should last no longer than fifteen or twenty minutes, for it was by paring the spectacle to twenty minutes or less that the series of scenes assumed a mechanical quality. Renewing the theatre in a mechanical process, Léger hoped to compete with the human spectacle on the streets and to provide modern man with an effective entertainment, a "distraction from...daily exhaustion."[19]

Another major problem with conventional theatre was the importance given to the "star artist," whom Léger described as "a frequent obstacle to unity."[20] Actors had always been a barrier to complete scenic homogeneity, their "authoritative personalities"[21] overstepping the group spectacle, their human material placing drastic restrictions on scenic objects, decor, and other means of scenographic expression. Léger expressed his sympathy for the star artist who, for centuries, conjured tricks and gimmicks in an unsuccessful attempt to elicit surprise and excitement from the audience, "but in spite of all his genius, he doesn't have a thousand different ways to smile, to turn, to fling out his leg, to leap."[22]

Léger advised the actor and dancer to search the environment, to discover the plastic and theatrical, or spectacular, value of objects; only in this way would they improve and renew their art. He suggested that the actor should be absorbed into the plastic matrix of a two-dimensional scenic landscape and that the scenery should be mobilized. Actors, dancers, and properties would then be integrated by a mechanical choreography, and the stage would acquire a physical and dynamic unity.

Once the human body and the plastic, mobile decor were joined, the importance and proportion of the human figure on stage would diminish. The actor would then function as a mechanism, as a *plastic means;* like every other piece of stage machinery, the performer became, in the Theatre of Spectacle, a "fixed value,"[23] no longer vulnerable to egotistical ambitions and no longer capable of wasting energy or action in pursuit of stardom. In the Theatre of Spectacle, the performer acquired maximum plasticity once he succumbed to the role of mobile scenery and realized that his value was no greater than that of any other object. The Theatre of Spectacle was first a spectacle of color, lights, icons, and moving objects.

Léger's theory was greatly influenced by his inveterate fondness for the circus. He admired "the strange architecture of colored tent poles, metallic rods, and ropes that cross[ed] each other and sway[ed] under the effect of the lights";[24] he also admired the acrobats and enjoyed the precision with which they performed their various stunts. Acrobats, he felt, performed at maximum efficiency and displayed in a single routine more "plastic passages"[25] than a corps of dancers in several scenes of ballet.

In the essay, "The Spectacle: Light, Color, Moving Image, Object-Spectacle," written in 1924, Léger described a hypothetical performance in the Theatre of Spectacle. He called for a shallow stage so that most of the movement and action would take place on the vertical plane. The background consisted of object-scenery which, like the human-scenery, was movable and participated in the stage action. Overhead, films were to be projected on the tops of the scenery and were to provide a backdrop for the mobile parts of the set. The film contributed to the animated stage since it showed luminous, metallic objects shifting and pulsating in air. The action consisted of six performers who crossed the stage turning cartwheels; the lights faded, and the performers returned as phosphorescent moving scenery on the dark stage. Léger's production, the object-spectacle, was a panorama of such effects and carefully timed activity. He warned technicians and performers that a plastic movement, a gesture, or a sound should not last two seconds longer than necessary; human faces were either concealed behind masks or makeup or held in expressionless, stiff, and metallic neutrality. The human material in the object-spectacle was to be "used in groups moving in a parallel or contrasting rhythm, on the condition that the general effect [was] in no way sacrificed to it."[26]

This description of an hypothetical performance revealed Léger's indebtedness to the circus, his insistence on plastic devices as a means to unifying the stage picture, and his conviction that only short, episodic acts or events were suitable for modern audiences. It was through acts such as those described above that the performance crossed the footlights, enthralled the audience, and restored to the theatre an inverse proportion between stage and auditorium.

The essay, "The Spectacle: Light, Color, Moving Image, Object-Spectacle," was written two years after Léger's work on the ballet *The Skating Rink* and approximately one year after his work on *The Creation of the World*. It is possible that these two commissions influenced Léger's concept of the spectacle.

The backdrop for Canudo's ballet, *The Skating Rink,* consisted of a semi-circular screen of curtains. The lower portion was, for the most part, left blank but dotted with two large spheres. Above the blank area, Léger painted enormous geometric, colored forms and broad lines. The dancers performed in front of the curtain, the brightly colored striped costumes making their bodies appear as silhouettes against the neutral, light curtain. Rischbieter remarks that when the performers danced, their silhouettes were "effects," presumably pictorial effects, against the curtain.

Despite the fact that the dancers appeared as special pictorial effects, there was little else in Léger's designs for *The Skating Rink* and in the production to indicate that Léger would, within two years, conceive a theory as radical as his theory for a Theatre of Spectacle. Perhaps the most influential and revealing work Léger undertook for the theatre, at least with regard to a Theatre of Spectacle, came later in the year, when Rolf de Maré commissioned Léger to design set and costumes for another production by the Swedish Ballet, *The Creation of the World*. In these designs, and in this production, Léger anticipated his Theatre of Spectacle.

The Creation of the World (1923)

In 1924, following the production of *The Creation of the World,* Léger voiced his admiration for Rolf de Maré, director of the Swedish Ballet, and Jean Borlin and his dancers, the troupe contracted to perform the ballet. Léger's homage to these artists expressed his delight with their artistic courage and foresight. He praised Rolf de Maré,

> ....the first person in France to have the courage to agree to a spectacle where everything is done with machinery and the play of light, where no human silhouette is on stage; and to Jean Borlin and his troupe, who are condemned to the role of moving scenery.[28]

Although Léger overstated the historical significance of this production in his praise and in the claim that the ballet dared "to impose on the public for the first time a truly modern stage, at least in terms of technical means,"[29] his zealous enthusiasm was certainly warranted; Léger undoubtedly saw the ballet as the manifestation of his concept of a modern entertainment. It was shortly after the production that Léger issued his manifesto on "The Spectacle."

A collaborative effort involving composer Darius Milhaud, librettist Blaise Cendrars, and Fernand Léger, *The Creation of the World* was based on a tale in African folklore about the day of creation. A pile of bodies, representing the chaos before creation, loomed in the center of the darkened stage. Moving very slowly behind the bodies were three deities — Nzame, Medere, and N'kava — performing a ritualistic ceremony over the heap of dormant beings. Gradually, the heap began to pulsate, and one by one, animals and plants emerged or sprouted from the central mass; then, figures representing Man and Woman rose up together, eye to eye, and danced the dance of desire and mating. The last creatures to be created were the wizards, magicians, witches, and other lowly characters; these joined in the circle of plants and animals and danced with the mating Man and Woman. The group eventually grew tired, and the pace of their orgiastic dance slackened, then stopped altogether. The creatures split up into small groups and exited, leaving the human couple alone to embrace and kiss.

On the proscenium stage of the Théâtre des Champs Elysées, Léger designed a modified wing and shutter system of painted panels that extended beyond and above the proscenium opening. The panels were placed three deep in staggered order, one behind the other at stage right, and two deep at stage left; four fly curtains were similarly placed overhead, the fourth concealing a rail or track for mobile scenery. At the rear of the stage, Léger painted an enormous backdrop and erected a tall monolithic wing on the far left downstage.

The hanging flats, panels, and monolith were painted in severe geometric forms, some depicting clouds and mountains in abstraction; the designs on the front panels consisted of bold geometric vectors. In effect, Léger's set was an adaptation of the techniques used in Analytic Cubism: Hard-edged, flattened geometric forms depicted the icons of a primieval setting. Other similarities to Analytic Cubist paintings included shifting scale, proportion, and perspective in the quasi-representational pattern of geometric forms; bold, fragmented shapes randomly ordered to disjoint space; and simultaneity.

Léger originally wanted to use inflatable skins to represent the non-human creatures and plantlife. The skins would have been filled with gas and sent aloft at the moment of creation. Darius Milhaud, however, pointed out the impracticality of this plan, noting that the noise of the pumps would have drowned out the music.[30] Léger then decided to mask the dancers' faces and bodies.

The costumes were conceived as classical African masks and sculpture. Léger believed that primitive communities employed the mask as a means to create spectacle; the mask not only concealed the human face but transformed it into a plastic object. African dancers realized they could bring about a "state of astonishment"[31] by turning the human figure into a plastic body. Following this example, Léger figured that a "state of astonishment" would reinforce the division between stage and auditorium and create a "fiction on stage."[32] To create a fiction on stage through plastic means was to create a spectacle.

Léger adapted the design of African masks in order to give the dancers' bodies the same spectacle value as the objects and scenery around them. Scenery and costumes were conceived in simplistic forms and painted in flat tones of yellow, ochre, deep blue, white, and black. Three twenty-six-foot placards were raised to depict the deities Nzame, Medere, and N'kava. These were flat, multi-colored constructions of geometric and linear forms; placed on the abstract designs were several realistically rendered features to indicate parts of the body: eyes, nose, horns, and cosmetic stripes, all painted to resemble the flat, abstract features on African masks. The three gigantic gods towered over the other figures on stage and were moved along the rails in the flies, parallel to the rear wall of the stage.

Measuring about half the height of the three twenty-six-foot gods were demi-gods shuffling about the stage on stilts. The mask for one of these characters simultaneously displayed a profile and frontal view of the head: the nose, mouth, and chin were seen in profile; the frontal view was distinguished from the profile view by a sharp diagonal line separating the head into two areas of light and dark tones. The torso was faceted into several flattened sections, each painted with a different abstract design. The demi-gods also moved in lines parallel to the rear wall.

Léger designed the costumes for the other characters in an identical fashion: by abstracting the anatomy in various geometric patterns. He succeeded in concealing the human figure and reducing the dancers to mobile objects and stage effects.

Rendering both decor and costumes in the same patterns, Léger pushed the performer into the plastic matrix of the set; mobilizing the enormous deities on rails and putting other characters on stilts, he eliminated the distinction between actor and scenery because the actor became a part of the scenery, his human proportions interpreted in plastic values. Léger managed to depersonalize Borlin's dancers and integrate their bodies into the choreography of scenic objects.

Writing in 1925, Léger proposed that the end of the spectacle was to create a "field for surprise,"[33] and to engender this surprise, the theatre artist needed to firmly integrate the mobile scenery and the human material so that the background, as well as the foreground, figures were given life. In this way, the spectacle would benefit from the "multiplication of means of effects"[34] and achieve an unparalleled unity in the formalistic synthesis of the mise-en-scène. This essay, "The Ballet Spectacle, the Object Spectacle," described the principles by which Léger conceived and executed the designs for Cendrars' ballet. The stage picture for *The Creation of the World* consisted of familial Cubistic forms multiplied many times over, then dispersed through space and ultimately bound in a two-dimensional, dynamic landscape. The interaction of foreground and background elements resembled the surface/depth dialogue contained in many of Léger's early Cubistic paintings.

Conclusion

Francis Fergusson referred not only to the theatre but to art in general when he wrote that "the very *idea* of a theatre" is to portray the spirit of the time and culture that formed it.[1] It is the ability of a work of art to reveal the character of its own age that makes art a document of the diachronic evolution of civilization.

Once considered an insubstantial adoration of primitivism, Cubism eventually became a portrait of the intellectual character of the modern age. When the Cubist painters penetrated the natural contours of objects and established the legitimacy of subjective perception over objective reality, they abandoned restrictions placed on painting by naturalism and perspectivism and embraced an attitude that became the hallmark of the twentieth century: the relativity of all perception, feeling, and thought. The Cubists' objective was not to paint a servile copy of nature but to invent a conceived reality through their paintings.

Cubism has become in retrospect the most formidable and influential artistic movement to have surfaced from the modern period because it created "a common standard or convention...underlying all realms of advanced contemporary thinking."[2] The Cubist vision, which dissected and reorganized perceived reality into a fictive reality of faceted lines, planes, volumes, and surfaces, served not only as a model for future literary and artistic practices but as a foreshadowing of the cinematic process in which reality was edited into a series of individual frames and images. The formal devices of the Cubist method created a paradigm for modern values, a paradigm to which all forms of contemporary art can be traced.

Paradoxically, Cubist painting was not primarily a theoretical activity. Picasso and Braque were usually reluctant to explain or intellectualize their work, preferring to concentrate on the act of painting. Their objective was to observe and interpret reality, then paint what they saw. As an historical and aesthetic elaboration of Post-Impressionism, Cubism has been explained as an "aesthetic pursuit,"[3] as something done. The Cubist painters dismantled and reassembled objects in reality and transferred their personal, painterly vision to the canvas.

The Cubist theatricians likewise principally concerned themselves with an "aesthetic pursuit" and inventing a conceived reality. The stage, like the canvas, became a surface for an aesthetic project, a radical interpretation of reality translated into stage icons. Like Picasso and Braque, Meyerhold and Tairov committed themselves first to the theatre as art, then to ideological or propagandistic messages. For this reason, Mordecai Gorelik claims that Meyerhold's major contribution was to reinstate the "theatre theatrical."[4]

In the Cubist theatre, the stage became central and was no longer treated merely as a platform for supporting actors or scenery. The stage and its various properties became integral components of the aesthetic convention of the theatre and were treated the way Cubist painters treated the canvas: not as vehicles for illusionism but as surfaces and materials to be activated and manipulated so that object and field interacted in space to create a totally homogenized pictorial space. As in Cubism, the end of this activity was to alienate — to distance — the viewer and establish the space as a formal part of the stage landscape.

Like Cubist painting, then, the Cubist theatre invented an aesthetic convention, a new formalistic vocabulary, to express the conceived theatrical reality. Like the painter, the theatre artist redefined objects in space. Where the painter's major interest was to translate his vision into shapes on canvas, the theatre artist concerned himself with transforming his Cubistic perceptions into gestures, sound, and scenography on stage. The theatre artist's primary concern was theatricalism, where the stage space became an independent, essential creative material to be organically fused with actors and props.

Cubism in art and theatre repudiated traditional concepts of production in its radical treatment of the interrelationship between objects and space. As in Cubist painting, space in the theatre — the mise-en-scène — was rendered in a formal synthesis. For Meyerhold, the stage was "strictly synthetical,"[5] and Tairov worked toward a synthesis of all theatrical elements in "an organic fusion of fundamentally related forms."[6]

Cubist painting and theatre were conventionalized means of filtering the most ordinary reality through the personal vision and whim of the artist and of producing a synthesis of paradigmatic forms normally seen in conflict with one another. While the painters sought to merge background with foreground and to dissolve the differences between substance and form, Cubist theatricians sought a visual synthesis through all aspects of production; the entire stage and cast became one form, one substance, one landscape, one formal synthesis. These practices created a new convention of staging or, as Léger wrote about all new art forms, invented a new realism.[7] All aspects of production were directed toward a Cubistic visual realization of the mise-en-scène.

Plates

Plate 1.   Georges Braque, *Houses at L'Estaque,* 1908

Plate 2.   Pablo Picasso, *The Reservoir, Horta de Ebro,* 1909.
Private Collection, New York

Plate 3.   Georges Braque, *Still-Life With Violin and Pitcher,*
1890–1910. Oeffentliche Kunstsammlung Basel

Plate 4.   Pablo Picasso, *Portrait of Daniel-Henry Kahnweiler,*
1910. Collection, The Art Institute of Chicago

Plate 5. Pablo Picasso, *Ma Jolie,* 1911–1912, Oil on Canvas, 39 3/8 x 25 3/4", Collection, The Museum of Modern Art, New York. Acquired through the Lillie P. Bliss Bequest.

Plate 6.   Pablo Picasso, *The Three Musicians,* 1921, Oil on Canvas, 6'7" x 7'3 3/4", Collection, The Museum of Modern Art, New York. Mrs. Simon Guggenheim Fund.

Plate 7. Kasimir Malevich, Front curtain design, 1913

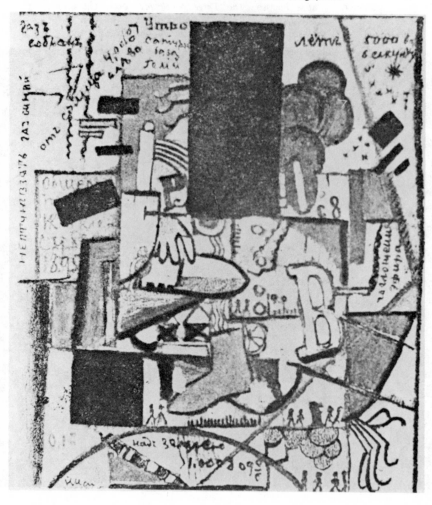

Plate 8. Kasimir Malevich, Backcloth for Act I, Scene I and Act
II, 1913

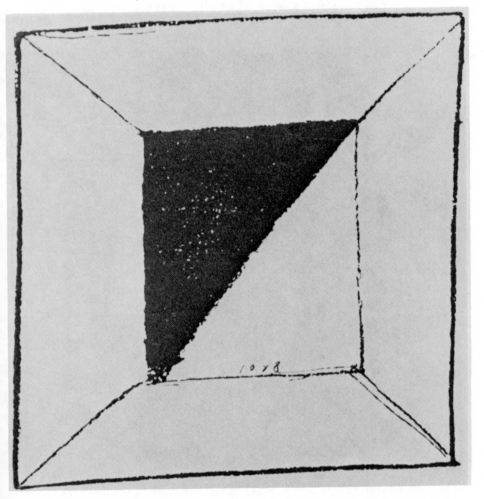

Plate 9. Kasimir Malevich, Backcloth for "Tenth Country" house, Act II, Scene VI, 1913

Plate 10. Kasimir Malevich, The composer Mikhail Matyushin (seated left), the artist Kasimir Malevich (seated right), and the playwright Alexander Kruchenykh (lying down), 1913

Plate 11. Kasimir Malevich, Costumes for Nero (upper left),
Futurecountry Strongman (upper right), The Squabbler
(lower left), and The Coward (lower right), 1913

Plate 12.   Natalia Goncharova, set for *Le Coq d'Or*, Act I, 1914

Plate 13. Pablo Picasso, The American Manager [(left) and The French Manager], from *Parade*. (1980 reconstruction after original of 1917), tempera on cardboard, wood, fabric, paper, metal and leather, 134 1/4 × 96 × 44 1/2". Collection, The Museum of Modern Art, New York.

Plate 14. A model for the setting for *Mystery Bouffe*, 1921

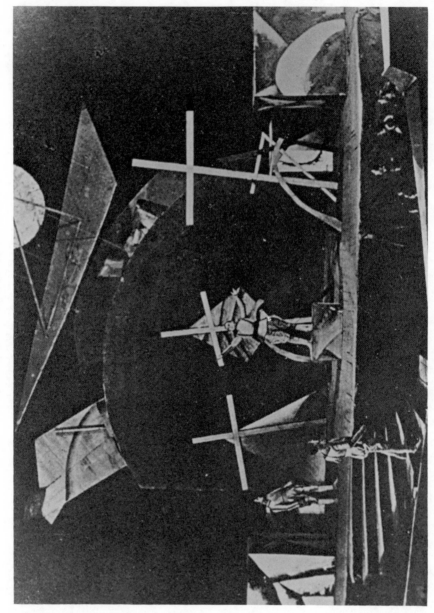

Plate 15. Setting for *The Dawns*, 1920

Plate 16.   Setting for *The Dawns*, 1920

Plate 17. Perceptual areas, *The Magnificent Cuckold,* 1928

Plate 18.   Movement as repetitions of formal patterns in the set piece, *The Magnificent Cuckold*, 1928

Plate 19. A homogenous landscape of geometric forms fused in space, *The Magnificent Cuckold*, 1928

Plate 20. Wooden apparatus for *The Death of Tarelkin*, 1922

Plate 21. The finale in *The Forest*, 1924

Plate 22.   The moving walls for *Give Us Europe*, 1924

Plate 23. A Moscow street scene, the mobile walls for *Give Us Europe*, 1924

Plate 24. Set for *Famira Kifared*, 1916

Plate 25. Sculptural presence in the groupings, *Famira Kifared*, 1916

Plate 26. Geometricized costumes, *L'Annonce Faite à Marie*, 1920

Plate 27. Alexander Vesnin, preliminary sketch of set for *Phaedre*, 1921

Plate 28.   Alexander Vesnin, sketch for Phaedre's costume, *Phaedre,*
1921

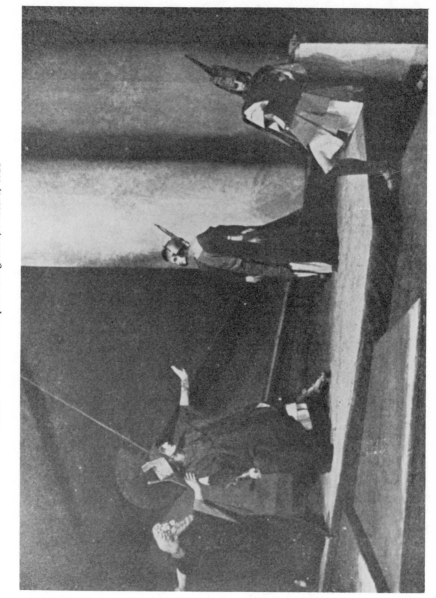

Plate 29. Geometricized pose and gesture, *Phaedre*, 1921

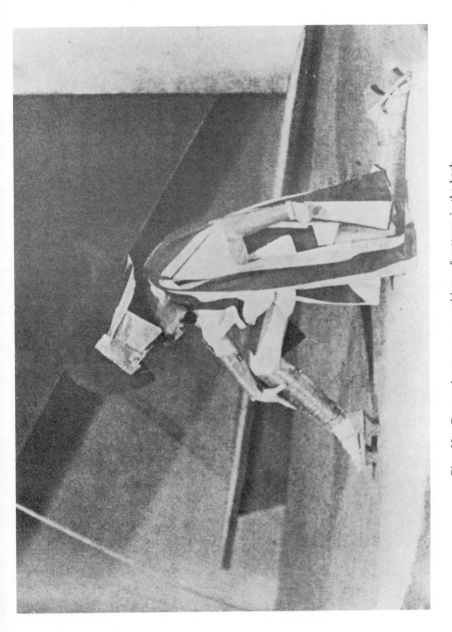

Plate 30.   Pose and gesture as repetitions of patterns in the background, *Phaedre*, 1921

Plate 31.   Fernand Léger, *The City*, 1919, Collection, Philadelphia Museum of Art, Philadelphia.

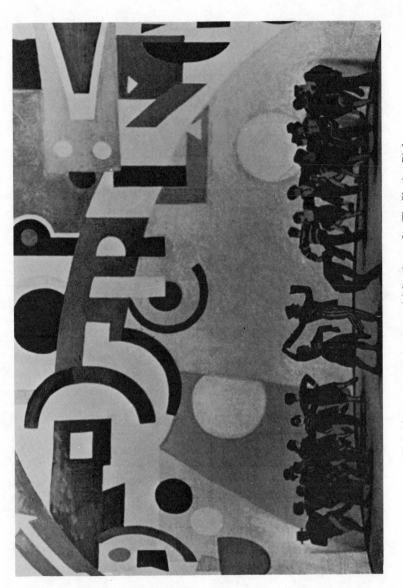

Plate 32.   Fernand Léger, a model for the set for *The Skating Rink*, 1922, Collection, Dansmusset, Stockholm.

Plate 33. The actual set for *The Skating Rink*, 1922

Plate 34.   Fernand Léger, a design (gouache) of the three deities,
The Creation of the World, 1923, Collection, Musee
Fernand Léger, Biot.

Plate 35. The set for *The Creation of the World*, 1923

Notes

Introduction

1. William Barrett, *Irrational Man* (Garden City, New York: Doubleday Anchor, 1958), p. 42.

2. Herschel Chipp, *Theories of Modern Art* (Berkeley, California: University of California Press, 1975), p. 193.

3. Paul Schwartz, *Cubism* (New York: Praeger Publishers, 1971), p. 135.

4. Paul M. Laporte, "Cubism and Science," *The Journal of Aesthetics and Art Criticism* 7 (March 1949)3:244.

5. Daniel-Henry Kahweiler, *The Rise of Cubism,* with an introduction by Robert Motherwell (New York: Wittenborn, Schultz, Inc., 1949), p. vii.

6. Schwartz, *Cubism,* p. 59.

7. Chipp, *Theories of Modern Art,* p. 260.

8. Ibid., p. 277.

9. See W. R. Fuerst and S. J. Hume, *Twentieth-Century Stage Decoration* (New York: Dover Publications, 1967) or Henning Rischbieter, ed., *Art and the Stage in the 20th Century* (Greenwich, Connecticut: New York Graphic Society Ltd., 1968).

Chapter 1

1. Paul Schwartz, *Cubism* (New York: Praeger Publishers, 1971), pp. 19-21.

2. Schwartz, *Cubism,* p. 39.

3. Fernand Léger, *Functions of Painting,* trans. Alexandra Anderson (New York: The Viking Press, 1965), p. 57.

4. Ibid.

5. Schwartz, *Cubism,* p. 46.

6. Daniel-Henry Kahnweiler, *The Rise of Cubism,* trans. Henry Aronson (New York: Wittenborn, Schultz, Inc., 1949), p. 14.

7. *Reviewing "Exposition Braque" at Chez Kahnweiler, 28 rue Vignon, Paris, for *Gil Blas,* 14 November 1908, Louis Vauxcelles wrote: "Monsieur Braque is a very daring

young man.... He despises form, reduces everything, places and figures, to geometrical schemes, to cubes. Let us not make fun of him, since he is honest. And let us wait" (Fry, *Cubism*, p. 50). Schwartz claims it was Braque's *Houses at L'Estaque* that inspired Vauxcelles' comment (Schwartz, *Cubism*, p. 39.)

8. Max Kozloff, *Cubism/Futurism* (New York: Charterhouse, 1973), p. 218.

9. Schwartz, *Cubism*, p. 7.

10. Herschel Chipp, *Theories of Modern Art* (Berkeley, California: University of California Press, 1975), p. 212.

11. Kahnweiler, *The Rise of Cubism*, pp. 11–12.

12. Kozloff, *Cubism/Futurism*, p. 55.

13. Chipp, *Theories of Modern Art*, p. 277.

14. William Barrett, *Irrational Man* (Garden City, New York: Doubleday Anchor, 1958), p. 44.

15. John Berger, *The Moment of Cubism and Other Essays* (London: Weidenfeld and Nicolson, 1969), p. 24.

16. Schwartz, *Cubism*, p. 49.

17. Kahnweiler, *The Rise of Cubism*, p. 7.

18. Chipp, *Theories of Modern Art*, p. 210.

19. Kozloff, *Cubism/Futurism*, p. 61.

20. Chipp, *Theories of Modern Art*, p. 223.

21. Gillaume Apollinaire, *The Cubist Painters: Aesthetic Meditations,* trans. Lionel Abel (New York: George Wittenborn, Inc., 1949), p. 13.

22. Ibid., p. 14.

23. Paul M. Laporte, "Cubism and Science," *The Journal of Aesthetics and Art Criticism* 7 (March 1949)3:244.

24. Ibid.

25. Ibid., p. 246.

26. Ibid., p. 255.

27. Berger, *The Moment of Cubism and Other Essays,* p. 23.

28. Edward Fry, *Cubism* (New York: McGraw-Hill, 1966), pp. 24–25.

29. Laporte, "Cubism and Science," p. 254.

30. Ibid., p. 246.

31. Kozloff, *Cubism/Futurism*, p. 103.

32. Laporte, "Cubism and Science," pp. 252–53.

33. Kozloff, *Cubism/Futurism*, p. 100.

34. Standish Lawder, *The Cubist Cinema* (New York, New York: University Press, 1975), p. 20.

35. Ibid., p. 7.

36. Ibid.

37. Ibid., p. 25.

38. Chipp, *Theories of Modern Art,* pp. 212–13.

39. Lawder, *The Cubist Cinema,* p. 20.

Chapter 2

1. Henning Rischbieter, ed., *Art and the Stage in the 20th Century* (Greenwich, Connecticut: New York Graphic Society Ltd., 1968), p. 137.

2. Mikhail Matyushin, "Futurism in St. Petersburg," *The Drama Review* (Fall 1971) (T-52):93.

3. Camilla Gray, *The Russian Experiment in Art: 1863–1922* (New York: Harry N. Abrams, Inc., 1962), p. 94.

4. Rischbieter, ed., *Art and the Stage in the 20th Century,* p. 137.

5. Gray, *The Russian Experiment in Art: 1863–1922,* pp. 150–51.

6. Ibid., p. 154.

7. Ibid., p. 278.

8. The list of Russian artists who worked with avant-garde producers includes Alexander Exter, Lazar Lissitzky, Liubov Poppova, Varvara Stepanova, Alexander Rodchenko, Vladimir Tatlin, and Georgy Yakulov.

9. Rischbieter, ed., *Art and the Stage in the 20th Century,* p. 137.

10. *The Drama Review* (T-52):104–05.

11. The first Futurecountryman spoke: "All is well that begins well!" The second asked, "What about the end?" The first answered, "There will be no end!" *The Drama Review* (T-52):97.

12. Ibid.

13. Ibid., p. 105.

14. Ibid.

15. *The Drama Review* (Fall 1971):93 referred to this sketch as the design for Act I, Scene I, and Act II, Scenes V and VI; *Art Forum* (December 1978):41 cited this same sketch as the backcloth for Act II, Scenes I and V.

16. Ibid., p. 114.

17. Ibid., p. 118.

18. Ibid., p. 120.

19. Ibid., p. 93.

20. Ibid., p. 104.

21. Rischbieter, ed., *Art and the Stage in the 20th Century,* p. 137.

22. Gray, *The Russian Experiment in Art: 1863-1922,* p. 186.

23. *The Drama Review* (T-52):109.

24. Rainer Crone "Malevich and Khlebnikov: Suprematism Reinterpreted," *Art Forum* (December 1978):40.

25. Rischbieter, ed., *Art and the Stage in the 20th Century,* p. 137.

26. *The Drama Review* (T-52):104.

27. Rischbieter, ed., *Art and the Stage in the 20th Century,* p. 137.

28. Ibid.

29. Crone, "Malevich and Khlebnikov: Suprematism Reinterpreted," p. 41.

30. *The Drama Review* (T-52):100.

31. Ibid., p. 96.

Chapter 3

1. Henning Rischbieter, ed., *Art and the Stage in the 20th Century* (Greenwich, Connecticut: New York Graphic Society Ltd., 1968), p. 82.

2. C. Spencer and P. Dyer, *The World of Serge Diaghilev* (Chicago: Henry Regnery Company, 1974), p. 90.

3. Guillaume Apollinaire, *Apollinaire on Art,* trans. Susan Suleiman (New York: The Viking Press, 1972), pp. 452-53.

4. E. T. Kirby, ed., *Total Theatre* (New York: E. P. Dutton & Co., 1969), p. xxiv.

5. Apollinaire, *Apollinaire on Art,* p. 452.

6. Neal Oxenhandler, *Scandal and Parade* (New Brunswick: Rutgers University Press, 1957), p. 48.

7. Lael Wertenbaker, *The World of Picasso, 1881-1973* (New York: Time-Life Books, 1977), p. 76.

8. Jean Cocteau, *Cock and Harlequin. Notes Concerning Music with a Portrait of the Author and Two Monograms by Pablo Picasso,* trans. Rollo Meyers (London: The Egoist Press, 1921), pp. 50-51.

9. Douglas Cooper, *Picasso Theatre* (London: Weidenfeld and Nicolson, 1968), p. 25.

10. Rischbieter, ed., *Art and the Stage in the 20th Century,* p. 82.

11. Paul Schwartz, *Cubism* (New York: Praeger Publishers, 1971), p. 145.

12. Max Kozloff, *Cubism/Futurism* (New York: Charterhouse, 1973), p. 103.

13. Rischbieter, ed., *Art and the Stage in the 20th Century,* p. 12.

14. Kirby, ed., *Total Theatre,* pp. 112-13.

15. Rischbieter, ed., *Art and the Stage in the 20th Century,* p. 76.

16. Kozloff, *Cubism/Futurism,* p. 103.

17. Ibid., p. 105.

18. Ibid., p. 109.

19. Cocteau, *Cock and Harlequin: Notes Concerning Music With a Portrait of the Author and Two Monograms by Pablo Picasso,* p. 272.

20. Cooper, *Picasso Theatre,* p. 25.

21. Margaret Crosland, *Jean Cocteau* (New York: Alfred A. Knopf, 1956), p. 52.

22. Cooper, *Picasso Theatre,* p. 25.

23. Rischbieter, ed., *Art and the Stage in the 20th Century,* p. 46.

24. Cooper, *Picasso Theatre,* p. 25.

25. Kirby, ed., *Total Theatre,* p. 86.

26. Roland Penrose, *Picasso: His Life and Work* (New York: Harper and Row, 1958, pp. 219–20.

Chapter 4

1. Meyerhold would frequently bring to rehearsals reproductions of paintings by Renoir, Manet, Degas, Memling, and Botticelli and use these to design scenery, props, costume, and actors' movement.

2. Edward Braun, ed., trans., *Meyerhold on Theatre* (New York: Hill and Wang, 1969), p. 174.

3. Norris Houghton, "Theory into Practice: A Reappraisal of Meierhold," *Educational Theatre Journal* 20 (October 1968):438.

4. Braun, ed., trans., *Meyerhold on Theatre,* p. 138.

5. Ibid.

6. Mordecai Gorelik, *New Theatres for Old* (New York: Samuel French, 1940), p. 188.

7. W. R. Fuerst and S. J. Hume, *Twentieth-Century Stage Decoration* (New York: Dover Publications, 1967), p. 46.

8. Braun, ed., trans., *Meyerhold on Theatre,* p. 134.

9. Ibid., p. 21.

10. James Symons, *Meyerhold's Theatre of the Grotesque* (Coral Gables, Florida: University of Miami Press, 1971), p. 54.

11. Braun, ed., trans., *Meyerhold on Theatre,* p. 166.

12. Ibid., p. 173.

13. Ibid.

14. Symons, *Meyerhold's Theatre of the Grotesque,* p. 45.

15. Braun, ed., trans., *Meyerhold on Theatre,* p. 205.

16. W. R. Fuerst and S. J. Hume, *Twentieth-Century Stage Decoration,* p. 57.

17. Nick Worrall, "The Magnificent Cuckold," *The Drama Review* 17 (March 1973) (T-57)1:27.

18. Edward Fry, *Cubism* (New York: McGraw Hill, 1966), p. 32.

19. Worrall, "The Magnificent Cockold," p. 28.

20. Ibid.

21. Max Kozloff, *Cubism/Futurism* (New York: Charterhouse, 1973), p. 83.

22. Worrall, "The Magnificent Cuckold," p. 30.

23. Nikolai Gorchakov, *The Theater in Soviet Russia,* trans. Edgar Lehrman (New York: Columbia University, 1957), p. 200.

24. Worrall, "The Magnificent Cockold," p. 29.

25. Ibid.

26. Ibid., p. 22.

27. Braun, ed., trans., *Meyerhold on Theatre,* p. 184.

28. Worrall, "The Magnificent Cuckold," p. 30.

29. Huntley Carter, *The New Spirit in the Russian Theatre, 1917–1928* (New York: Benjamin Blom, Inc., 1970), pp. 67–68.

30. Worrall, "The Magnificent Cuckold," p. 16.

31. Fry, *Cubism,* p. 20.

32. Ibid., p. 14.

33. Worrall, "The Magnificent Cuckold," p. 33.

34. Ibid., p. 24.

35. Symons, *Meyerhold's Theatre of the Grotesque,* p. 131.

36. Worrall, "The Magnificent Cuckold," p. 19.

37. Ibid., p. 27.

38. Fernand Léger, *Functions of Painting,* trans. Alexandra Anderson (New York: The Viking Press, 1965), p. 41.

39. Worrall, "The Magnificent Cuckold, p. 22.

40. Ibid.

41. Ibid., p. 30.

42. Daniel-Henry Kahnweiler, *The Rise of Cubism,* trans. Henry Aronson (New York: Wittenborn, Schultz, Inc., 1949), pp. 11–12.

43. Braun, ed., trans., *Meyerhold on Theatre, p. 186.*

44. E. T. Kirby, ed., *Total Theatre* (New York: E. P. Dutton & Co., 1969), p. 137.

45. Braun, ed., trans., *Meyerhold on Theatre,* p. 186.

46. Ibid.

47. Ibid.

48. Ibid., p. 187.

49. Ibid., p. 186.

50. Fry, *Cubism,* p. 20.

51. Symons, *Meyerhold's Theatre of the Grotesque,* p. 92.

52. Ibid., p. 93.

53. Paul Schwartz, *Cubism* (New York: Praeger Publishers, 1971), p. 59.

54. Braun, ed., trans., *Meyerhold on Theatre,* p. 137.

55. Ibid., p. 322.

56. Ibid.

57. Gorchakov, *The Theatre in Soviet Russia,* p. 207.

58. Ibid.

59. Carter, *The New Spirit in the Russian Theatre,* p. 212.

60. Symons, *Meyerhold's Theatre of the Grotesque,* p. 115.

61. Norris Houghton, *Moscow Rehearsals* (New York: Octagon Books, 1975), p. 93.

62. William Tucker, *Early Modern Sculpture* (New York: The Oxford University Press, 1974), p. 70.

63. André van Gyseghem, *Theatre in Soviet Russia* (London: Faber and Faber Ltd., 1943), p. 19.

64. Gorchakov, *The Theater in Soviet Russia,* p. 208.

65. Symons, *Meyerhold's Theatre of the Grotesque,* p. 122.

66. Gorchakov, *The Theater in Soviet Russia,* p. 209.

67. Ibid., p. 193.

68. Ibid., p. 209.

69. Symons, *Meyerhold's Theatre of the Grotesque,* p. 121.

70. Schwartz, *Cubism,* p. 23.

71. Worrall, "The Magnificent Cuckold," p. 28.

72. Braun, ed., trans., *Meyerhold on Theatre,* p. 142.

Chapter 5

1. Alexander Tairov, *Notes of a Director,* trans. Wm. Kuhlke (Coral Gables, Florida: University of Miami Press, 1969), p. 47.

2. Ibid.

3. Ibid., p. 77.

4. Ibid., pp. 115–16.

5. Ibid., p. 109.

6. Ibid., p. 111.

7. Ibid., pp. 114–15.

8. Mikhail Zelikson, *The Artists of the Kamerni Theatre* (Moscow, 1935), p. xxxiv.

9. Tairov, *Notes of a Director,* p. 112.

10. Norris Houghton, *Moscow Rehearsals* (New York: Octagon Books, 1975), p. 119.

11. W. R. Fuerst and S. J. Hume, *Twentieth-Century Stage Decoration* (New York: Dover Publications, 1967), p. 77.

12. John Bowlt, *Stage Designs and the Russian Avant-Garde (1911-29),* Introduction to the Exhibition Catalog (Washington, D.C.: International Exhibitions Foundation, 1976), p. 8.

13. Ibid., pp. 7-8.

14. Ibid., p. 8.

15. Tairov, *Notes of a Director,* p. 112.

16. Ibid.

17. Zelikson, *The Artists of the Kamerni Theatre,* p. xxiv.

18. Ibid.

19. Bowlt, *Stage Designs and the Russian Avant-Garde 1911-29),* pp. 8-9.

20. Huntley Carter, *The New Spirit in the Russian Theatre, 1917-1928* (New York: Benjamin Blom, Inc., 1970), p. 85.

21. Ibid.

22. Tairov, *Notes of a Director,* p. 112.

23. Zelikson, *The Artists of the Kamerni Theatre,* p. xxxii.

24. Ibid.

25. Ibid.

26. Tairov, *Notes of a Director,* p. 124.

27. Ibid., p. 115.

28. W. R. Fuerst and S. J. Hume, *Twentieth-Century Stage Decoration,* p. 77.

29. Nikolai Gorchakov, *The Theater in Soviet Russia,* trans. Edgar Lehrman (New York: Columbia University, 1957), p. 227.

30. Ibid.

31. Zelikson, *The Artist of the Kamerni Theatre,* p. xxxiv.

32. Ibid.

33. Ibid.

34. Gorchakov, *The Theater in Soviet Russia,* p. 227.

35. Houghton, *Moscow Rehearsals,* p. 119.

36. Zelikson, *The Artists of the Kamerni Theatre,* p. xxxiv.

37. Gorchakov, *The Theater in Soviet Russia,* p. 227.

38. Mordecai Gorelik, *New Theatres for Old* (New York: Samuel French, 1940), pp. 295-98.

Chapter 6

1. Fernand Léger, *Functions of Painting,* trans. Alexandra Anderson (New York: The Viking Press, 1965), p. 82.

2. Max Kozloff, *Cubism/Futurism* (New York: Charterhouse, 1973), pp. 40-43.

3. Standish Lawder, *The Cubist Cinema* (New York, New York: University Press, 1975), p. 70.

4. Henning Rischbieter, ed., *Art and the Stage in the 20th Century* (Greenwich, Connecticut: New York Graphic Society Ltd., 1968), p. 92.

5. Kozloff, *Cubism/Futurism,* p. 43.

6. Lawder, *The Cubist Cinema,* pp. 69-70.

7. Ibid., pp. 67-69.

8. Léger, *Functions of Painting,* p. xiii.

9. Ibid., p. 52.

10. Ibid., p. 72.

11. Rischbieter, ed., *Art and the Stage in the 20th Century,* p. 97.

12. Léger, *Functions of Painting,* pp. 72-73.

13. Ibid., p. 39.

14. Ibid.

15. Ibid., pp. 39-40.

16. Ibid., p. 35.

17. Rischbieter, ed., *Art and the Stage in the 20th Century,* p. 97.

18. Léger, *Functions of Painting,* p. 36.

19. Ibid., p. 38.

20. Ibid., pp. 38-39.

21. Ibid., p. 71.

22. Ibid., pp. 38-39.

23. Ibid., p. 73.

24. Ibid., p. 40.

25. Ibid., p. 39.

26. Ibid., pp. 40-41.

27. Rischbieter, ed., *Art and the Stage in the 20th Century,* p. 98.

28. Léger, *Functions of Painting,* p. 41.

29. Ibid., pp. 41-42.

30. Rischbieter, ed., *Art and the Stage in the 20th Century,* p. 98.

31. Ibid., p. 97.

32. Léger, *Functions of Painting*, p. 38.

33. Ibid., p. 72

34. Ibid.

Conclusion

1. Francis Fergusson, *The Idea of a Theater* (Princeton, New Jersey: Princeton University Press, 1949), pp. 1-2.

2. Paul M. Laporte, "Cubism and Science," *The Journal of Aesthetics and Art Criticism* 7 (March 1949)3:244.

3. Max Kozloff, *Cubism/Futurism* (New York: Charterhouse, 1973), pp. 4-5.

4. Mordecai Gorelik, *New Theatres for Old* (New York: Samuel French, 1940), p. 303.

5. Edward Braun, ed., trans., *Meyerhold on Theatre* (New York: Hill and Wang, 1969), p. 138.

6. Alexander Tairov, *Notes of a Director,* trans. Wm. Kuhlke (Coral Gables, Florida: University of Miami Press, 1969), p. 84.

7. Fernand Léger, *Functions of Painting,* trans. Alexandra Anderson (New York: The Viking Press, 1965), p. 114.

Bibliography

Apollinaire, Guillaume. *Apollinaire on Art*. Translated by Susan Suleiman. New York: The Viking Press, 1972.

————. *The Cubist Painters: Aesthetic Meditations*. Translated by Lionel Abel. New York: George Wittenborn, Inc., 1949.

Apollonio, Umbro, ed. *Futurist Manifestos*. Translated by Brain, Flint, Higgitt and Tisdall. New York: The Viking Press, 1973.

Appia, Adolphe. *The Work of Living Art & Man Is the Measure of All Things*. Translated by H. D. Albright. Coral Gables, Florida: University of Miami Press, 1960.

Ball, Hugo. *Flight Out of Time*. Translated by Ann Raimes. New York: The Viking Press, 1974.

Barr, Alfred, Jr. *Cubism and Abstract Art*. New York: The Museum of Modern Art, 1936.

Barrett, William. *Irrational Man*. Garden City, New York: Doubleday Anchor, 1958.

Berger, John. *The Moment of Cubism and Other Essays*. London: Weidenfeld and Nicolson, 1969.

Bergson, Henri. *Creative Evolution*. Translated by Arthur Mitchell. New York: Henry Holt & Company, 1911.

Bowlt, John. *Diaghilev and Russian Stage Designers*. Introduction to the Exhibition Catalog. Washington, D.C.: International Exhibitions Foundation, 1972.

————. *Stage Designs and the Russian Avant-Garde (1911-29)*. Introduction to the Exhibition Catalog. Washington, D.C.: International Exhibitions Foundation, 1976.

Braun, Edward, ed., trans. *Meyerhold on Theatre*. New York: Hill and Wang, 1969.

————. *The Theatre of Meyerhold: Revolution on the Modern Stage*. London: Eyre Methuen, 1979.

Carter, Huntley. *The New Spirit in the Russian Theatre 1917-1928*. New York: Benjamin Blom, Inc., 1970.

Chipp, Herschel. *Theories of Modern Art*. Berkeley: University of California Press, 1975.

Cocteau, Jean. *Cock and Harlequin: Notes Concerning Music With a Portrait of the Author and Two Monograms by Pablo Picasso*. Translated by Rollo Meyers. London: The Egoist Press, 1921.

Cooper, Douglas. *Picasso Theatre*. London: Weidenfeld and Nicolson, 1968.

Craig, Edward Gordon. *The Art of the Theatre*. Edinburgh and London: T. N. Foulis, 1905.

————. *Scene*. New York: Benjamin Blom, Inc., 1968.

Crone, Rainer. "Malevich and Khlebnikov: Suprematism Reinterpreted." *Art Forum* (December 1978):38-47.

Crosland, Margaret. *Jean Cocteau*. New York: Alfred A. Knopf, 1956.

Esslin, Martin. *The Theatre of the Absurd*. Rev. ed. Garden City, New York: Doubleday Anchor, 1969.

Fergusson, Francis. *The Idea of a Theatre.* Princeton, New Jersey: Princeton University Press, 1949.

Fry, Edward. *Cubism.* New York: McGraw-Hill, 1966.

Fuerst, W. R. and Hume, S. J. *Twentieth-Century Stage Decoration.* New York: Dover Publications, 1967.

Goldberg, Rose Lee. *Performance, Live Art 1909 to the Present.* New York: Harry N. Abrams, Inc., 1979.

Gorchakov, Nikolai. *The Theater in Soviet Russia.* Translated by Edgar Lehrman. New York: Columbia University, 1957.

Gordon, Mel. "German Expressionist Acting." *The Drama Review* 19 (September 1975): 34–50.

Gorelik, Mordecai. *New Theatres for Old.* New York: Samuel French, 1940.

Gray, Camilla. *The Russian Experiment in Art: 1863–1922.* New York: Harry N. Abrams, Inc., 1962.

Hoffman, Hans. *Search for the Real and Other Essays.* Rev. ed. Cambridge: MIT Press, 1967.

Hoover, Marjorie. *Meyerhold: The Art of Conscious Theater.* Amherst: University of Massachusetts Press, 1974.

Houghton, Norris. *Moscow Rehearsals.* New York: Octagon Books, 1975.

————. "Theory into Practice: A Reappraisal of Meierhold." *Educational Theatre Journal* 20 (October 1968).

Kahnweiler, Daniel-Henry. *The Rise of Cubism.* Translated by Henry Aronson. New York: Wittenborn, Schultz, Inc., 1949.

Kirby, E. T. "The Mask: Abstract Theatre, Primitive and Modern." *The Drama Review* 16 (September 1972):5–21.

————, ed. *Total Theatre.* New York: E. P. Dutton & Company, 1969.

Kirby, Michael. *Futurist Performance.* New York: E. P. Dutton & Company, 1971.

Kozloff, Max. *Cubism/Futurism.* New York: Charterhouse, 1973.

Laporte, Paul M. "Cubism and Science." *The Journal of Aesthetics and Art Criticism* 7 (March 1949):243–256.

Law, Alma. "Meyerhold's Woe to Wit." *The Drama Review* 18 (T-63) (September 1974) 3:89–107.

Lawder, Standish. *The Cubist Cinema.* New York, New York: University Press, 1975.

Léger, Fernand. *Functions of Painting.* Translated by Alexandra Anderson. New York: The Viking Press, 1965.

Markov, Pavel. *The Soviet Theatre.* New York: Putnam's Sons, 1935.

McLuhan, Marshall. *Understanding Media: The Extensions of Man.* New York: McGraw-Hill, 1964.

The Moscow Kamerny Theatre. Moscow: Inturist, 1936.

Nicoll, Allardyce. *The Development of the Theatre.* 5th ed. New York: Harcourt Brace Jovanovich, 1966.

Oxenhandler, Neal. *Scandal and Parade.* New Brunswick: Rutgers University Press, 1957.

Peckham, Morse. *Man's Rage for Chaos.* Philadelphia: Chilton Books, 1965.

Penrose, Roland. *Picasso: His Life and Work.* New York: Harper and Row, 1958.

Read, Herbert. *A Concise History of Modern Painting.* New York: Praeger Publishers, 1974.

Rischbieter, Henning, ed. *Art and the Stage in the 20th Century.* Greenwich, Connecticut: New York Graphic Society Ltd., 1968.

Roose-Evans, James. *Experimental Theatre from Stanislavsky to Today.* Rev. ed. New York: Universe Books, 1973.

Schmidt, Paul. "A Director Works with a Playwright: Meyerhold and Mayakovsky." *Educational Theatre Journal* 29 (May 1977):214–220.

Schwartz, Paul. *Cubism*. New York: Praeger Publishers, 1971.

Simonson, Lee. *The Stage Is Set*. New York: Theatre Arts Books, 1963.

Spencer, C. and Dyer, P. *The World of Serge Diaghilev*. Chicago: Henry Regnery Company, 1974.

Steegmuller, Francis. *Cocteau: A Biography*. Boston: Little, Brown and Company, 1970.

Symons, James. *Meyerhold's Theatre of the Grotesque*. Coral Gables, Florida: University of Miami Press, 1971.

Tairov, Alexander. *Notes of a Director*. Translated by Wm. Kuhlke. Coral Gables: University of Miami Press, 1969.

Tucker, William. *Early Modern Sculpture*. New York: The Oxford University Press, 1974.

van Gyseghem, André. *Theatre in Soviet Russia*. London: Faber and Faber Ltd., 1943.

"Victory Over the Sun." *The Drama Review* 15 (T-53) (Fall 1971)4:93–122.

Wertenbaker, Lael. *The World of Picasso, 1881–1973*. New York: Time-Life Books, 1977.

Wiener, Leo. *Contemporary Drama of Russia*. Boston: Little, Brown and Company, 1924.

Worrall, Nick. "The Magnificent Cuckold." *The Drama Review* 17 (T-57) (March 1973) 1:14–34.

Zelikson, Mikhail. *The Artists of the Kamerni Theatre*. Moscow, 1935.

Index